Early Years Play and Learning

How can you create an effective play and learning environment for young children?

This practical book provides an accessible framework for observing and assessing children's learning through play. It will help early years practitioners to deepen their understanding of the links between intellectual development, the growth of language and the emotional well-being of young children.

Drawing on many years of research and working with teachers, the author has developed the Social Play Continuum, a unique observation tool and a means of monitoring and developing a child's social progress through skills such as problem-solving, investigation and imaginative discourse. This tool forms an integral part of this innovative text, offering practitioners in a wide range of early years settings a means of focusing their observations of play. In addition, the book aims to:

- support the development of 'areas of provision';
- illustrate progression from 'associative' to 'cooperative' play;
- consider links with the Foundation Stage Curriculum, Profiling and the National Curriculum;
- acknowledge the many constraints that have operated on early years practitioners in the past decade.

Blending theory and practice, this book is aimed at all early years practitioners concerned with quality provision for their pupils. It is also the ideal text to support student teachers and undergraduates on Early Childhood Studies degrees, and classroom assistants.

Pat Broadhead is Research Professor for Education at Northumbria University.

Early Years Play and Learning

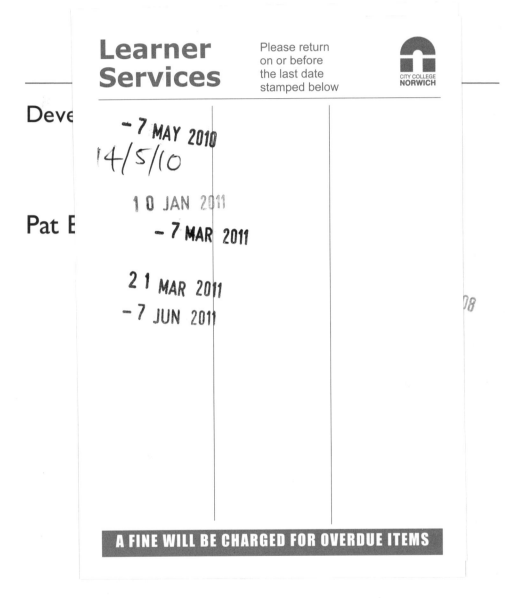

Learner Services

Please return on or before the last date stamped below

CITY COLLEGE NORWICH

Deve

– 7 MAY 2010

14/5/10

10 JAN 2011

– 7 MAR 2011

21 MAR 2011

– 7 JUN 2011

Pat E

A FINE WILL BE CHARGED FOR OVERDUE ITEMS

RoutledgeFalmer
Taylor & Francis Group

LONDON AND NEW YORK

First published 2004
by RoutledgeFalmer
11 New Fetter Lane, London EC4P 4EE

Simultaneously published in the USA and Canada
by RoutledgeFalmer
29 West 35th Street, New York, NY 10001

Reprinted 2004

RoutledgeFalmer is an imprint of the Taylor & Francis Group

© 2004 Pat Broadhead

Typeset in Baskerville and Gill by BC Typesetting, Bristol
Printed and bound in Great Britain by
TJ International Ltd, Padstow, Cornwall

British Library Cataloguing in Publication Data
A catalogue record for this book is available from the British Library

Library of Congress Cataloging in Publication Data
A catalog record for this book has been requested

ISBN 0–415–30339–7

To Dave, Matthew and Tom; best players in the world

Contents

This book is supported with photocopiable resource material available on the following website: www.routledgefalmer.com/teacher.

You can download copies of the Social Play Continuum from this site to support your observations.

In addition, a number of professional development activities have been devised around materials included in this book. These can also be downloaded from the website for immediate use by teacher trainers, by staff in schools and by all early years practitioners.

Acknowledgements

I should like to thank the children, teachers and heads who, over the years, have allowed me into their play, their classes and their schools, especially those who have worked with me most recently and intensively. Thank you for taking risks, for your patience, your participation and your insights; especial thanks to Jenny for naming the 'whatever you want it to be place'. Thanks to the many colleagues along the way who have given encouragement and feedback, to Kathy Sylva for her interest and encouragement in the early days and to Angela Anning for suggesting that language and action needed separating. Thanks to Carolyn and Penny for persuading me that publication was possible and giving some sound advice in Spetses.

Introduction

Background

My interest in young children's sociability and cooperation began almost 25 years ago. Having left school at 16, when I trained as a teacher I was in the last cohort to be accepted without A Levels. Consequently I could qualify as a teacher not with a degree, but with a Certificate in Education. I took my B.Ed. as a part-time degree and in that three-year period, Matthew and Tom were born. Over the coming years, along with many, many observations in early years settings and in reception and year one classrooms, Matthew, Tom and their friends were to be a great source of knowledge in deepening my interest in and understanding of the growth of sociability and how it might be facilitated.

For that first degree I became interested in rough and tumble play. Before becoming a mother, and as a teacher in a nursery setting, I had been thinking about the extent to which the resources and activities we provided for children could encourage them to be sociable. It seemed to me that much of what we traditionally offered encouraged solitary achievement and that children had to find opportunities to be sociable and cooperative somewhere in the spaces in between. They were quite good at finding those spaces, and rough and tumble play was an important activity for them; however, in my early days as a teacher, along with my colleagues in the nursery setting, I seemed to spend quite a lot of time trying to stop the rough and tumble. This set me thinking, and gave me a focus for my first piece of research, the dissertation for the B.Ed.

In the two nurseries where I undertook the data collection, I observed play on the climbing frame, running and chasing play and any indoor episodes of spontaneous rough and tumble that occurred. It was during these very early observations that I became aware of the importance of facial expressions, eye contact and smiling and laughter for young children seeking to make new contacts and to establish friendships. I also noted how difficult it was for such contacts to be sustained for those children who did not, for whatever reason, know how to use such facial gestures. The work of Blurton-Jones (1967, 1972), an ethnographer, was influential at this time; he looks in some detail at rough and tumble play also. I saw how quickly children became skilful at making and following their own rules so as to bring order and structure to their play. I became interested in how play themes emerged, almost from nowhere it seemed at first, although I gradually came to recognize the themes as clear indicators of thinking in action and began to recognize how the themes were taken up and developed by the children, becoming a unifying focus for their social and cooperative interactions.

Sometimes there seemed to be a form of telepathy among the children who, with apparently few verbal clues, identified and sustained a unifying theme that gave meaning to their play and their interactions but which wasn't always apparent to me as observer.

The nursery staff had agreed not to intervene in any play that I was watching and I had said that I would intervene only if I felt that children were unhappy or in danger. Consequently, during these first observations, the children were probably allowed to develop their play for longer periods, uninterrupted, than might otherwise have been the case. What surprised me was that I never had to intervene in the ongoing play. The most alarming event I recall was when a play tunnel was blocked off by two children (one at each end) with one child still inside. The trapped child began to cry and as I stood, a girl called to the two 'trappers', 'Let her out, she's crying'. They did so; the crying girl was consoled. Then she smiled and said 'Let's do it again' and went back into the tunnel – beginning to conquer her fears perhaps. This was the first of many, many surprises that my observations were to bring. It took me a while to realize (I won't say how many years, it's too embarrassing) that being surprised actually meant that I was learning something new about children's learning processes. It becomes apparent in Chapter 4, in the section 'Puppies, baths, toilets and washing machines', that I can still be substantially surprised by children, which shows that I still have a good deal left to learn.

Having been bitten by the observation bug, I sought to deepen my understanding of the complexities of becoming sociable and cooperative for Master's work. I moved beyond rough and tumble play and broadened the range of activities under observational scrutiny to those traditionally provided (Broadhead, 1997). There were 11 such activities in focus at this point. For the research into rough and tumble play, I had used an observational schedule developed by Charlesworth and Hartup (1967). Building on the earlier research, for this second study, I redesigned this schedule, drawing a distinction between 'communicatory elements' and 'cognitive elements' (Broadhead, 1997). Looking back at this listing now, the distinctions seem artificial in the form that they took at this stage in the ongoing research. But at this point, I was grappling with a means of making the cognitive aspects of cooperative activity explicit. I was analysing the detailed observational notes to try to identify how children were acting and interacting and how they were using language as they played. This listing was a step along the way to understanding and articulating the complexities of their play, allowing me to be increasingly systematic as an observer and allowing me to begin to illustrate the interrelationship between language and cognition when children play together. At this point, I used the communicatory–cognitive listings as an *aide-mémoire* and taped the narrative of the observations for later transcription. Data analysis showed how individual behaviours were seen to cluster and sequence as children played. From this further analysis came the first version of the Social Play Continuum, the observational tool at the heart of this book (Broadhead, 1997). This clustering and sequencing subsequently became the basis for the four domains of the Continuum that are introduced and explained in some detail in Chapter 2 and elsewhere in the book. But, first of all, there is a little more to tell in the story of its development.

Cosaro's work (1985) illustrates how children become protective of their play, not through selfishness or an unwillingness to share, but because they are seeking some degree of control to withstand constant interruptions to their play from adults and other children. Linked to this, ongoing observations had shown how objects were central in sustaining play and how resolving conflict relating to the ownership of objects was a key factor in relation to whether play continued or ceased. I was beginning to realize that very often, children needed time to build momentum in their play, and in building momentum they became sociable and then cooperative (the distinctions between 'sociability' and 'cooperation' will become clearer as the book unfolds). These early observations were revealing how the giving and receiving of objects made an important contribution to increasing or diminishing the levels of sociability and cooperation. This aspect also linked to children being protective of the objects. The objects were strongly associated with play continuity. Continuity seemed important for building momentum.

The impact of interruptions in children's play was to become more evident when the research moved into reception classes. This further developed my understanding of the need for time for momentum to build and for children to develop high levels of reciprocity between interacting peers. The levels of interruption were greater in reception classrooms as children were called away to do their work for the teacher more frequently than had been the case in nursery settings. I began to see that the greater the number of interruptions and, along with this, the fewer the opportunities for play, the more resourceful children had to become in finding the 'spaces' to play in.

Chorpita and Barlow (1998) have explored the development of anxiety in children and its links with the extent of personal control in the early learning environment. They tentatively suggest that diminished control may foster a cognitive style that interprets teaching–learning activities as being out of one's control to shape or influence. In this way, the young child then becomes separated from the construction of the curriculum. It becomes constructed around them and for them but, as individuals in this learning environment, they may have fewer and fewer points of contact with their own cognitive agenda (Moss and Penn, 1996). The culture of access to play began to change in reception classrooms as 'infant teachers, after an initial angry reaction to the proposals for a National Curriculum simply knuckled down to making the best compromises they could' (Anning, 1997:105). The continuing impact on opportunities to play, and to become sociable and cooperative through play, are explored in some detail in Chapter 1.

The next phase in the development of the Social Play Continuum was through observations in two receptions classrooms. This second phase used the existing Social Play Continuum to focus the observations, rather than the listings adapted from Charlesworth and Hartup (1967). It seemed important to shift the focus to slightly older children so as to see how their maturity and experience impacted on their play through their use of language and action. I deliberately selected classrooms where, despite the emerging climate of literacy and numeracy influences on routines and timetabling, the teachers were aiming to sustain free play access for reception children. This was the only way it would be possible to access peer interactions with traditionally available activities. There were five Areas of Provision in focus in this second phase, the same five in focus in this book – sand, water, role play, large and small construction, and small world. These are introduced in Chapter 1.

It was after this second phase of research that the Continuum emerged as two sheets rather than one (Broadhead, 2001). The first sheet remained focused on language and action. Whereas previously I had presented the interrelationships between language and action in terms of clustered behaviours, this later phase of research introduced notions of **reciprocity** between interacting peers, linking the increase in reciprocity with associated increases in cooperation. Along with a deeper understanding of reciprocity came an understanding of **momentum**. The Continuum had four **levels** at this point in time (these have now become **domains** for reasons explained a little later): *Level 1*, Associative Play; *Level 2*, Social Play; *Level 3*, Highly Social Play; and *Level 4*, Cooperative Play. I was becoming increasingly interested in how we could support children's progression across the levels and beginning to see the Continuum's potential as a tool to support practitioners in supporting children's learning through play. As noted above, observations revealed that the children's play needed to gather momentum so as to progress across the levels – they often needed time to build that momentum, particularly if they were not too familiar with one another. It became possible to recognize, within the children's interactive behaviours, a point at which they might be making a **transition** to a higher (or lower) level of play. (These transitions are illustrated in Broadhead, 2001.) Gathering momentum was linked with the degree of reciprocity – an elaboration of what had previously been referred to as 'clustering and sequencing'.

The second sheet of the Social Play Continuum that emerged from this phase of the research was concerned with describing 'the socio-cultural characteristics' of the play. Vygotsky's work and that of related authors are important reference points for this research and are examined in greater detail in Chapter 4. Vygotsky (1986: 206) emphasizes the social orientation of cognitive development: 'what the child is able to do in collaboration today, he will be able to do independently tomorrow'. In grappling with ideas about the influence of the social dimension on learning, I sought to synthesize from the observational data the salient socio-cultural characteristics of play at each of the four levels (domains) of the Continuum. A key point to emphasize here is that the majority of the observational data has come from classrooms where white, Western cultural traditions were in the majority. This is not to suggest that white Western culture is not complex and multifaceted, rather to make clear some inevitable limitations of data collection thus far in this research. The second sheet also aimed to support the observer in setting the observations in the broader context of the play as a whole experience for children – focusing on language and action in the first instance (sheet 1) and then rebuilding the observed play into its socio-cultural context to see it as a whole experience for the interacting peers (sheet 2).

Throughout the observations, I had been interested solely in peer interactions. The research has never been concerned with observing teacher–pupil interactions. The intention was to better understand and so be able to describe in detail what sociability and cooperation looked like when children were given opportunities to engage with it for extended periods. Nevertheless, it was always important that the work would be useful and accessible to practitioners. This aspect came to the fore in the third phase of research, undertaken with reception teachers and which is being substantially reported in this publication. Various chapters also examine how the Social Play Continuum links with current debates and demands for planning in relation to the Stepping Stones and Early Learning Goals and for pupil assessment in relation to Foundation Stage Profiling. The Social Play Continuum, along with traditional Areas of Provision, does, I believe, have the potential to link planning and assessment through systematic observation.

Back to my sons and back in time for a moment to the earlier days of research. Matthew and Tom began rough and tumbling themselves, with one another and with a wide range of friends of different ages. Watching them all at play I began to recognize the extent of children's sensitivity to the comfort and safety of others while still playing quite vigorously. I made efforts to look at their vigorous behaviour through the eyes of a researcher rather than a mother, trying to be impartial sometimes rather than always being emotionally involved, looking at behaviour and interaction rather than seeing the potential for danger. The more I watched, the more I began to feel differently about what I saw.

Where once I had seen aggression, I began to see the testing of physical limits, mainly for boys, but also for some girls. Where once I had seen hostility, I began to see enjoyment of physical contact with some degree of intimacy as boys rough and tumbled. My perspective was changing as my understanding of the male psyche deepened. I know from the many presentations I have given of my work, that many female teachers remain concerned about the perceived levels of violence in boys' interactions, at the ways in which mock fights seem to quickly become 'real' fights in the adults' eyes. I do not want to seem dismissive of these concerns here; these are complex matters. Head (1999:35) writes: 'Each boy joining a group starts with his own agenda and lack of empathy with others'. There are clear distinctions to be drawn between getting to know strangers and growing up with siblings. In trying to deepen my own understanding of how children become sociable and cooperative, it has also been important to consider how the perspectives of the adults around them shape and influence the children's emerging (or otherwise) capacity for being sociable and cooperative. Chapter 4 considers some of these gender issues in a little more detail.

Phase 2 of the research had identified *four levels* of the Continuum. When the reader is introduced to the Continuum in Chapter 2, s/he will see reference to *four domains*. This deliberate change of terminology was made for three reasons.

1   In order to distance the research from the use of the term 'levels' in National Curriculum and testing parlance. The term 'level' now has connotations associated with apparent ability in relation to preconceived targets. The language, actions and characteristics of the Social Play Continuum are *not* developmental targets. They are points of reference which illustrate how young children combine the use of language and action so as to sustain their sociable and cooperative encounters.
2   To distance the research from ideas about and understandings of 'stages of development'. The word 'continuum' has been deliberately selected to promote a sense of unification when reflecting on aspects of children's learning, rather than one of disparity.
3   To distance the research from ideas about and understandings of 'readiness to learn'. Chapters 4 and 5 argue for supporting children as co-constructors of thecurriculum, alongside adults, for recognizing their own, vibrant capacity for knowing when thinking and doing are connecting them to new ways of seeing the world around them. Let's put them back 'in control' alongside practitioners in structuring and enjoying their early years learning environments.

Something that this research has shown very clearly is that the resources, the repeated opportunities for peer engagement, the organizational aspects and the types of adult intervention affect the levels of sociability as much as and perhaps more than the individual level of achievement of any child. It's not that children can't be sociable; rather that, if we always consign them to 'playing in the spaces' they have few opportunities for developing their social skills and along with this, there are few opportunities for adults to deepen their own understandings of how children become sociable – a double whammy, we might say.

The research has shown that individual children may play and interact with different degrees of sociability and cooperation at different times and with different peers and different materials. It has been known for children to operate in one domain of sociability during one observation and in another domain during another observation. Neither response would be seen as evidence of progression or regression in their overall development – but studying their responses can help us to better understand the nature of learning. These understandings were further developed once the research moved into year one classrooms, and some of these findings and examples are described and discussed also.

Promoting practitioner research – beyond watching children

This publication wants to promote the paradigm and support the practice of researching play in mainstream classrooms and early years settings for everyone responsible for supporting learning – nursery nurses, pre-school workers, teachers and teaching assistants. I have tried to demonstrate my commitment to this by showing how research has impacted on my own knowledge and understanding over time, rather than to exhort others to do it because I think it's a good idea. Of course, lots of people think it's a good idea; it's a great idea and these aspects are explored in more detail in Chapter 3.

In this introduction, I have also briefly referenced insights gained from observing my own children at play. There's a real danger of being inappropriately anecdotal and a little cringe-making when talking about your children or your grandchildren in this way. Just like Jean Piaget, we women love to talk about our children, don't we? There *are* distinctions to be drawn between systematic study and anecdotal reflection, although each has its own kind of impact. The reason I make no apology for referencing my children in this introduction, and the reason I suspect so many of us do draw upon our home-based anecdotes, is that these are powerful learning experiences for each of us, as we accumulate information and develop new understandings of the learning process. Almost everyone who works with young children becomes a constant watcher of children. We do it on beaches and in shopping malls. Our eyes are taken by children's activities because we are, without always being conscious of the fact, seeking to deepen our personal knowledge of the learning process. In watching other people's children and our own, we extend our points of reference for connecting their language and action as indicators of their learning. It is an intellectual enterprise. However, I would argue that the impact of the enterprise is far less substantial if we only 'watch'. The new knowledge and the new understandings come from combining structured observations with post-observation reflection. To embed our new knowledge, adults need to do what children need to do – to talk with others, to be cooperative, to deepen our understanding in communities of learners.

What Vygotsky (1986) claimed for children also applies for adults, and I would slightly alter the quote above to read: 'what the adult is able to understand in collaboration today, s/he will be able to act upon independently tomorrow'.

Chapter 1

Areas of Provision in early years settings

Building on our heritage in the early years

Areas of Provision are well established within curricular experiences for young children in this country, although more substantially perhaps, in nurseries and playgroups where play-based approaches to teaching and learning have more traditionally allowed children to use all their senses when learning. Sand, water, large and small construction, small world and role play have, for a long time, been taken for granted as essential for supporting young children's learning. In each of these areas of play and exploration, the young child, alone, with adults and with peers, can direct their play and expand their understandings of how the world works and of how they can have influence within and upon that world.

It seems important to think beyond the actual 'materials' themselves (sand, water, bricks, etc.) and to consider how these long-established play opportunities relate one with another and with other resources – hence the use and exploration of the term 'Areas of Provision' in the book. It may be that these play opportunities are so taken for granted that there's been a tendency to 'provide them' but not to focus to any great extent on their ongoing development and enhancement. In addition, as is discussed a little later in the chapter, their very existence as play opportunities may have been threatened by many of the enforced changes that have arisen from substantial legislation over the past 15 years and its subsequent long-term impact on schools, nurseries and playgroups (David *et al.*, 1993; David, 1999).

Sand and water play have long been associated with the development of mathematical and scientific knowledge in the early years curriculum. Associated mathematical and scientific vocabulary can be introduced, practised and understood alongside the tipping and pouring and the scooping and sifting.

Sand and water are natural media and are recognized as having strong therapeutic properties (for adults as well as for children). Brierley (1993) points out that while modern children have many visual experiences in their early years of growth and development, tactile experiences are often more limited. At this age, texture is 'important and fascinating'. He reminds us that 'children's exploring fingers are an extension of their eyes' (p. 60) and through tactile experiences young children learn to discriminate. Also, sand and water can become settings for imaginative and fantasy-based activity. Given a range of types of play resources from which to choose, a water tray can become a shop and a sand tray can be used to retell familiar stories from books, television and cinema – and vice versa. They enable children to revisit and relive their social and cultural experiences and events. Through these resources we can bring the outside indoors in a country renowned for inclement weather.

Having researched in and visited many Norwegian classrooms, it was interesting to note that these Areas of Provision (sand and water) seldom made an appearance indoors; this illustrates the importance of recognizing the impact of tradition on our provision. In Norway, it seems that they are absent from classrooms because (despite what we might consider their inclement weather) Norwegian children spend considerable amounts of time outdoors and it is here that they dig and wade, investigate and explore. Educators there may feel that children do not need the outdoors brought indoors in a small-scale way. Teachers I have worked with who did bring the outdoors in in this way did begin to see benefits for children. They began to observe that the ways in which children played with water indoors were different from outdoor play because of the smaller scale. Despite outdoor access, indoor play was popular with the children who would continue outdoor themes but also play more interactively with peers, perhaps encouraged by the closer physical proximity around the tray. The teachers observed, in particular, that the children's play allowed them to connect emotional expression with physical and imaginative engagement. The following scenario illustrates some of this in a small way. It was a scenario that I observed over several days while working with two Norwegian teachers making a video on aspects of classroom organization and planning.

In Siv's classroom, in northern Norway, a six-year-old boy, new to the class and the local area, was having great trouble settling into the daily routines. He withdrew himself from class activity regularly and disrupted from a distance. He wandered around the room, disrupting others as they worked and played. On the day we introduced the water tray, he headed for it straight away. He played in a solitary way for much of the time but as Siv watched and listened, she saw his clear preoccupation with the boats and heard his occasional discussion with others about his father who was away fishing in the Lufoten Islands. After his water play, he approached Siv, who was with a group of children in the writing area. He said he wanted to draw a picture of his father on his boat. Because Siv now knew of these circumstances, based on her observations, she was able to chat to him about his father. The boy agreed that he missed his father and talked about when he thought he would return. He drew his picture and wrote a few words. He then walked around the room, smiling and talking to other children and showing them his picture. Soon, many of the children in the class, as well as Siv, knew about his father. This activity had drawn him into the class community in a small but seemingly important way. Siv remarked, later in the week, that his disruptive behaviour had diminished from that point. He began to respond more positively when she drew him into whole class discussions and he also talked more freely and regularly about his father. He began to make a book for his father for when he came home from fishing.

This scenario illustrates the therapeutic qualities of such play along with its potential to link into other areas of learning and knowledge.

In relation to the origins of *construction play*, at the turn of the century, in European kindergartens, Froebel's 'gifts' were demonstrating the potential of wooden bricks in nurturing children's mathematical knowledge and problem-solving skills. Building on Froebel's work and ideas, Gura (1992:31) gives us a detailed illustration of the power of block play in contributing mathematically and scientifically to children's learning as they simultaneously master three-dimensional space and develop their understanding of physical balance, structural integrity and visual harmony. As well as illustrating the aesthetic properties of block play, Gura details its capacity for allowing children to represent ideas non-verbally and symbolically. Children are 'natural improvisers' (p. 123). In relation to block play, Gura identifies a phenomenon that teachers and I noted in our observations of children in all Areas of Provision. She likens it to the way communications are exchanged between dancers, choreographers and their audience:

> Meanings are passed on, picked up and negotiated between individuals or between members of a group and even between groups, who share understandings of the system and the kinds of things that can be said with it.
>
> (p. 42)

The teachers and I also spoke of 'a kind of telepathy' that very focused, cooperating children seemed to have. They seemed to need few words to share their common vision. There were occasions when we observed their play for some time without knowing what it was that the children were building because they seemed to have passed the need to discuss it with one another. Such examples are illustrated in Chapter 3.

Small world resources and role play meet imaginative and emotional needs (as of course do sand, water and construction). They allow the child to represent and relive the familiar and the unfamiliar. A child can re-engage, in a personally controlled way, with experiences and events that have made them fearful, anxious, angry, happy, curious and pleased. Susan Isaacs' beliefs-in-action in the Maltings School continue to open our minds to the young child's emotional life. Her philosophy about free expression underpinned children's experiences and, as Drummond (2000) points out in her re-examination of Isaacs' beliefs and practice, there was virtually no constraint on children's verbal expression nor on their intellectual impulses. Their expressions of infantile sexuality, their anal and urethral interests and their feelings (including anger and aggression) along with their views on everything around them were all allowed expression.

As Drummond goes on to discuss, Isaacs recognized the importance of connecting the affective with the cognitive – the emotional with the intellectual – an inter-connectedness with much currency in present-day thinking about the nature of learning across all age groups, adults as well as children.

It is likely that Isaccs would see modern-day provision for emotional expression as a dilution of her own philosophies. Undoubtedly and perhaps inevitably we have become more pragmatic and constrained in what we do and offer in present-day settings. As Drummond (2000) notes, in modern-day early years settings, we are more constrained by conventions to select for our attention those aspects of children and of childhood that fit our hopes and dreams for children and for society. Susan Isaacs was clearly an exceptional individual in many ways, willing to take risks and push back boundaries in the interests of young children's development.

Many of today's early years educators also aim to offer as many opportunities as possible for children's emotional expression alongside opportunities for authentic and comprehensive investigation and question-raising by children. Some educators may be prepared and able to push back the boundaries further than others. As this research has shown, and as later chapters will illustrate, supportive head teachers were essential for the teachers involved in this research to become willing to reintroduce Areas of

Provision into their reception and Year 1 classrooms in the face of what they saw as a prevailing preoccupation with 'formal learning' and 'attaining set standards'. As Dowling (1995) notes, the early years 'sensitive' head may find it easier to be supportive than do head teachers whose experience is mainly with older children.

In briefly introducing these Areas of Provision, it is not the intention to establish their isolation, one from another, in educators' minds. Rather, it is:

- to recognize and build on our early years, educational traditions and heritage with a timely refocusing on the development of Areas of Provision in early years settings
- to begin to make explicit the distinctive yet interrelated contributions from within and across the Areas of Provision in supporting children's social, emotional and intellectual growth
- to recognize these Areas for their potential to assist educators in their finely tuned and well-focused observations of children at play
- drawing on their observations of children at play, to then assist educators in developing their Areas of Provision in creative and informed ways.

Let us move on to consider briefly some aspects that might have inhibited the creative development of Areas of Provision in early years settings in more recent years.

The early years in a changing world

Since the 1944 Education Act, and until very recently, the provision of nursery education had been at the discretion of a local authority. This led to wide regional variations in levels of nursery provision in this country (DES, 1990; National Commission on Education, 1993). It was not until the Children Act of 1989 that local authorities were required to make provision, in this case, for children in need and including those not yet in school. Almost ten years later, the 1998 Education Act required local authorities to make sufficient places available so as to ensure that five half-days of free provision would be available for all four-year-olds – this was the first time that statutory provision had been made for four-year-olds in England and Wales. This legislation was followed by similar provision for three-year-olds, beginning in 2000 in areas of economic disadvantage. These initiatives are funded by the government, through local authorities.

From the mid-1980s onwards, the educational world has experienced massive changes across all age ranges. This has required primary schools to engage in multiple innovation management (Wallace, 1991) through their increasingly focused engagement with school development planning (Broadhead et al., 1996; 1998). Numerous Education Acts in a comparatively brief period (compared to other, similar periods in history) have ensured that momentum was maintained in the pace of change in primary schools. Anyone who has worked in schools throughout this period would not doubt that managing and surviving change have been the order of the day for some time.

During this period, change was impacting on providers for young children in other ways. Playgroups, established as a temporary measure in the 1960s, became widely established as the anticipated expansion of provision for young children recommended by the Plowden Report (CACE, 1967) and the Framework for Expansion (under Margaret Thatcher as Secretary of State for Education in 1978) failed to materialize. From 1998 onwards, playgroups have become established as mainstream providers and local authorities are charged with ensuring (via the Early Years Development and Childcare Partnership, EYDCP) that local playgroups are sustainable and are staffed by suitably qualified personnel – bringing considerable new responsibilities and demands to voluntary sector workers.

The 1990s also saw a rapid expansion of private nurseries as they too recognized the need to fill the gaps in areas where statutory services were insufficient for young children and families. Women were returning to work in greater numbers, or returning after maternity leaves, families were seeking dual incomes where possible and as we moved into the millennium, opportunities for and levels of interest in Lifelong Learning were increasing. Local authorities, via the EYDCP, acquired similar responsibilities in relation to private providers to those they had for the voluntary sector in ensuring that three- and four-year-olds receive their entitlement for their five half-days (or $12\frac{1}{2}$ hours) of free provision in a 'quality' environment.

The High/Scope work in the USA had long been reporting its findings to show that early interventions, via good quality pre-school experiences that actively involve parents, have a positive impact (see Schweinhart *et al.*, 1993; O'Flaherty, 1995). One of the most enticing aspects of these findings for government, as they began to permeate consciousness on this side of the Atlantic, was that early intervention could save money later on, in costly interventions relating for example to family break-up, teenage pregnancies and levels of criminality. This research was to impact on Labour policy from 1998 onwards, after the publication of *Meeting the Childcare Challenge* (DfEE, 1998a) and a plethora of related initiatives aimed at intervention, including the establishing of Early Excellence Centres and Sure Start initiatives across the country, further initiatives to be overseen and coordinated by the EYDCPs.

The educational legislation that has impacted on how we make provision for younger children includes the 1986, the 1988 and the 1992 Education Acts. These respectively introduced Local Management of Schools, a National Curriculum and its assessment and the Monitoring and Inspection of Schools, with the first Monitoring and Inspection Framework for nursery and primary schools following a few years later (OfSTED, 1995).

As head teachers and chairs of governors began to manage their budgets in the late 1980s and on into the early 1990s they came to see, very clearly, the value of a four-year-old in a context of funding formulas. Young children have a relatively high monetary value in many formulas for funding. In relative terms, across the primary age range, four-year-olds bring a substantial premium into the school. Their presence in school also secures future funding for the school at an early stage in the child's school career. The early 1990s saw some pressures on parents, by some head teachers, to admit children early to school 'in order to secure their place'. Despite the fact that the 1944 Education Act requires that a child should be in full-time education 'at the beginning of the term after the term in which they are five', by 1995 estimates of around 75 per cent of four-year-olds and non-statutory five-year-old children were being quoted. Being prior to legislation relating to class sizes for reception and Key Stage 1 children (this legislation was to be in place by September 2000), these pre-school aged children could find themselves in classes of 35 or more children with only one adult to care for and educate them (Oberhuemer and Ulich, 1997).

From the late 1980s and into the early 1990s, studies had begun to illustrate some of the dangers for young children in this potentially premature engagement with formal learning and extensive teacher-directed activity (Bennett and Kell, 1989; DES, 1989; Cleave and Brown, 1991). Sylva (1991) identified the phenomenon of 'too formal too soon' and went on to point out the dangers of the 'overly academic curriculum' limiting opportunities for young children to be self-determining and self-directing in their learning.

Another outcome of the 1986 and 1988 Acts and the devolution of funding to schools was, as predicted, to place them within a competitive, market-forces-led climate. The publication of league tables from 1992 onwards and the associated local and national press coverage sealed the fate of schools as being intent on achieving the highest grades possible at the end of Key Stage 2 tests by ensuring that they 'met their targets', 'improved their standards', 'demonstrated their effectiveness', and remained competitive.

This accountability climate was subsequently strengthened by the requirement for local education authorities (LEAs) to submit their Educational Development Plan in which they outlined to government, via the Department for Education and Skills (DfES), how they would raise standards across the schools within their local authority (Broadhead *et al.*, 1999). This related to a number of areas in focus for improvement but, first and foremost, to improving standards in literacy and numeracy. This was of course in line with the then Secretary of State for Education's intention to reach national targets of pupil achievement in literacy and numeracy by September 2002. These targets were for 75 per cent of children to reach level 4 in their maths end of Key Stage 2 tests and 80 per cent to meet level 4 in their English end of Key Stage 2 tests. This prevailing climate required primary school heads to engage in a dialogue with their LEA relating to their individual targets and subsequently to think about ways and means of achieving these targets in order to demonstrate and defend their effectiveness. Relatively large periods of school time were already being devoted to maths and literacy. This has long been a tradition in English primary schools, but never before had these subjects been the focus of attention in such a marked climate of public accountability and talk of 'failing schools' or 'schools with serious weaknesses'.

The literacy and numeracy initiatives were never statutory. However, paralleling as their introduction did the first extended wave of Ofsted Inspections, it was assumed by schools that they would need to be clearly evident across all classrooms to bring about a successful inspection. Lacking clear guidance on the matter, this was also assumed to apply to reception classrooms – the youngest children in formal education. Who was about to risk testing the requirement through omission? Probably not the vast majority of schools which, by 1999, had implemented the Literacy Hour.

The following quote is taken from a reception teacher, interviewed before we began the joint research in reception classrooms. This clearly illustrates the dilemmas for teachers evident by the late 1990s:

> Most of the morning is taken up with literacy and numeracy now isn't it? The difficulty is trying to balance what is expected from the curriculum and all the other important things which you are having to try and put into two hours in the afternoon. It is a tension. I'm wanting to be with them and near them and watch what is going on and learn how to develop it more and yet sometimes I feel that I can't because I must be getting on with the other things.

Another reception teacher involved in the research illustrated how, in her view, this prevailing climate of target setting had pushed her towards inappropriate provision for these younger children:

> I feel that I am being pushed in many ways by target setting, of getting the children to a certain standard, ready to access National Curriculum at Level 1. I feel as though I am pushed by the government in one way – you must get children doing this – but feel that little children shouldn't be doing this until they are ready. I do feel that we push children into formal work far too early and I hope that the review of the Early Learning Goals will bring more flexibility for reception teachers, to interpret the curriculum in a way that suits the needs of children.

Later in this interview this teacher reiterated her point made above, that these levels of formality in teaching styles were not meeting young children's learning needs:

> as a teacher I have to be looking to get that balance right so that they are moving forward academically but also ensuring all their needs are being met in the class- room . . . it tears my heart sometimes because I think these little children shouldn't be sitting here doing this.

Pascal (1990), Bennett *et al.* (1997) and Wood and Bennett (2000) have demonstrated in their research how reception teachers might espouse the principles of play as crucial to development and learning but that these principles are often absent in practice within their classrooms. It would seem that the years of change had done little to improve the quality of experiences for many of the young children who were finding themselves in reception classrooms.

Much has been written about the Ofsted Inspection process and its impact on schools, notably the high levels of stress that accompanied the first and second waves of inspec- tion (Jeffery and Woods, 1996, 1998; Fitz-Gibbon and Stephenson-Forster, 1999; Case *et al.*, 2000). It has been claimed that 'inspection lowers morale, exhausts teachers and leads to a lull in post-inspection development in schools in the longer term' (Case *et al.*, 2000:16). High levels of stress inevitably diminish creative thinking. In addition, the preoccupation with league tables alongside the fears of being labelled a 'failing school' or a 'weak teacher' led to an increasing emphasis on teacher-led activity in younger age groups, largely because teachers thought that this was what the Inspector would want to see on entry to the classroom.

The phenomenon of the 'under-achieving boy' emerged in this country around the turn of this century, partly from the analysis of literacy scores and also fuelled by media stories of diminishing success in public examinations. This perspective quickly gained acceptability (Wood, 2000) and seemed to resonate with many reception teachers' experiences of four- and five-year-old boys 'unable to sit still' for their literacy and numeracy work. The reasons for this were unlikely to be poor parenting, low intel- ligence or an inability to concentrate but were rather the inappropriateness of many of the teacher-directed tasks in this overly formal climate in relation to the child's social, emotional, physical and intellectual needs at this point in the growth of body and mind.

Play, in the forms of the Areas of Provision with which this book is concerned, rapidly began to disappear from the classrooms of younger children. Many teachers felt that it was difficult to justify play-based learning and alongside this, and understandably, their focus was elsewhere in the curriculum, steeped as they were at this point in talk of standards, targets and failing schools. The comments above from research participants illustrate the prevailing dilemmas that the teachers of young children were facing, especially in reception classrooms.

There were two crucial, related elements to consider. Firstly, where schools had nursery classes attached, the top-down pressure to prepare children for the formality of teacher-led activity later in their school life began to impact at a level perhaps never before seen in the history of nursery education in this country. Secondly, initial teacher training courses had received their required competences and standards in Circular 4/98 (DfEE, 1998b). These clearly focused on training new teachers to deliver subject knowledge, across the age range. They were much criticized for failing to take sufficient account of the importance of personal professional knowledge about the nature of learning in the early years. Although later revisions were made and the potential for an Early Years Specialist emerged in later revisions to the training standards, substantial numbers of beginning teachers were emerging from training institutions with con- siderably greater experience of implementing the literacy and numeracy hours in a reception classroom than in organizing, providing, structuring and observing play- based learning. Initial training experiences leave a powerful legacy in establishing fundamental principles of action to inform future practices – for better and for worse.

We do seem to be 'emerging from under' but established norms and associated behaviour change only slowly, unless of course they are legislated for and brought to account in very public ways. The Desirable Learning Outcomes (what kind of language was that for describing children's learning?) have been superseded by the Foundation Stage Curriculum with its Early Learning Goals and age-related stepping stones – more of this in Chapter 3. The Foundation Stage Curriculum encompasses the period from three years to the end of reception year. It gives status to the early years by formally recognizing this as a crucial learning period, yet it has been pointed out that four and five years of age may be inappropriately young for beginning formal schooling (Broad- head, 1995a; Moss and Penn, 1996; Anning, 1997), recognizing these early years as a continuum of learning with no substantive transitions taking place until well after five years of age. Six and seven years of age are well-recognized transitional ages in other European countries and are currently subject to scrutiny in Wales.

In addition, the Qualifications and Curriculum Authority (QCA) has now recog- nized the value of observation for practitioners working with young children and implementing professional development opportunities linked to this area. The reception teacher who pleaded above for time to 'watch what is going on and learn how to develop it' may begin to find herself in a climate more conducive to this important activity as the century unfolds. Observation is moving centre stage in early years settings. However, given the prevailing climate, it has to be acknowledged that educators may come to see observation as yet another imperative foisted upon them by policy-makers, another new task through which they will subsequently be held accountable. Other research projects have demonstrated how focused observations can be a crucial dimension within educa- tors' professional development repertoires, notably the Effective Early Learning Project

(EEL) (Pascal *et al.*, 1994, 1995, 1996) and Laevers' work which focuses through observation on deep-level learning and involvement in young children (Laevers, 1993, 1994, 1996).

Ofsted inspections are becoming 'light touch' and, associated with this, the construct of the 'self-evaluating' school is beginning to see the light of day. This may move the prevailing climate away, perhaps, from one of accountability to a professional ownership of development and improvement – time will tell. The EYDCPs are now shining the spotlight on, among other things, making quality provision for young children across all settings – although debates about and definitions of quality are not unproblematic areas (Balageur *et al.*, undated; Moss and Pence, 1994). These debates are being informed through findings from the EPPE (Effective Provision of Pre-School Education) project, a major longitudinal study of a range of early years settings (see Sylva *et al.*, 1999b and many subsequent publications from the research team). All of this is providing a much-needed return to an agenda concerned with the place of play in children's learning. Once again, it may become legitimate to think about sand and water, about large and small construction, about role play and imaginative play, and about their respective contributions to children's learning in a thoughtfully structured and informed learning environment where children's needs and interests are legitimate factors in curriculum construction.

Illustrating Areas of Provision – some scenarios

When this research began in nursery settings, many years ago, the decision to focus on these particular areas was taken because it was felt that here would be some of the best opportunities for watching children play with their peers in relatively uninterrupted and free-flow play. If it was going to be possible to chart the growth of sociability on into cooperation, then a considerable body of observational data would be required. As becomes evident later, there are clear implications for adult intervention in children's play so as to promote the growth of social and cooperative skills. However, in the first instance it was important to focus on what children did when left alone to do it in areas where there seemed to be some potential for cooperation to occur.

The period of research discussed in this chapter, in five reception classes, was funded jointly by University departmental research funds and by the Local Educational Authority. The University money provided five half-day periods of supply cover for each teacher. This allowed some non-contact time for the teachers so that they and I could, together, undertake paired observations in each of the Areas of Provision. These paired observations were followed by reflective discussions on what we had observed. While we did use a developing version of the observational schedule (the Social Play Continuum) that is introduced in the next chapter, the following scenarios do not include any specific references to the schedule. Rather the intention here is 'to get a feel' for aspects of it and to really focus on children at play.

The LEA money allowed the teachers to purchase some additional resources to support their focus on Areas of Provision. One teacher who did not have small world resources in the classroom purchased these so that this play could be included in our observations. Another, already convinced that block play was highly beneficial, bought additional bricks; another reception teacher invested in a larger water tray. Another invested in storage space as she had come to see how important easy access to a good range of resources was in giving children good opportunities to extend their ongoing play. The reception teachers were supported in selecting these purchases by an early years adviser from the LEA who also believed that Areas of Provision should be celebrated rather than hidden.

This section is designed and presented with three purposes in mind:

1   to help the reader to 'get a feel' for how the Social Play Continuum was developed and refined, through the identification of recurring play behaviours and uses of language and the contextual characteristics of social and cooperative play
2   to illustrate the important interrelationship between the basic material (sand, water, etc.) and additional resources that children might access in relation to the emergence and progression of play themes
3   to identify links between Areas of Provision and the six areas of learning within the Foundation Stage Curriculum.

Let us look at some contexts where this was happening as children played with their peers. Each of the following scenarios is taken from a reception classroom for children aged four and five in the foundation stage of learning. In this section also, the five schools, the head teachers and the reception teachers involved with research are introduced. Each of the head teachers and the reception teachers was interviewed before our joint observations of children's play began. Building on the extracts provided earlier in this chapter, we hear a little more from each of them as to something of the constraints they have experienced and beliefs they have about the best ways to support children's learning in the early years. We hear also from the head teachers about their hopes from participation in the research project.

Opportunities for children's engagement with the six areas of learning in the Foundation Stage Curriculum are identified as follows:

- personal, social and emotional development – **PSE**
- communication, language and literacy – **CLL**
- mathematical development – **MD**
- knowledge and understanding of the world – **KUW**
- physical development – **PD**
- creative development – **CD**.

An explanatory narrative is offered on the right-hand side of the scenario description. This narrative also incorporates reference to the behaviours and characteristics which make up the Social Play Continuum to be examined more thoroughly in the forthcoming chapters. Just to reiterate, the Continuum has four domains:

- Domain 1: Associative
- Domain 2: Social
- Domain 3: Highly Social
- Domain 4: Cooperative.

Scenario 1: Heartland Primary School

Area of Provision: Role Play, the Home Corner
Domains on the Continuum: Mainly Social with some Associative

---

Heartland is a recently amalgamated primary school with 410 pupils and 14 staff. In the head's words (Kate) it has 'mixed catchments with a bias towards private housing'. At the time of the research there were 30 children in the reception class. Rose, the reception teacher, had been at the school for six years and worked with the reception class for the previous four years. She was also deputy head of the school. She had originally trained as a junior/secondary teacher and after the birth of her own children had retrained on a 'junior/infant conversion course . . . I started to be interested in children and what made them tick.'

When asked what she hoped for from the school's involvement in the research, Kate, the head, had replied:

> I hope that it's doing it already, really, making us focus because of the area we chose. A major priority is to look at role play and the interactions that go on there. But I'm also looking forward to meeting with other colleagues in other schools, with early years people.

Rose, the reception teacher had remarked:

> I want to be able to focus in and observe children because that is just a luxury that we don't often have. Occasionally we have had students in and I have been able to do that. I know we should be able to timetable times when we can just observe but it doesn't always happen.

This observation of the home corner lasted 15 minutes; two girls were already playing when the observation began. During the play, one girl and one boy came into the home corner. After we had observed, Rose and I identified this play as mainly *Social* (Domain 2 of the continuum) and occasionally *Associative* (Domain 1 of the Continuum).

1.35: Two girls are in the home corner. One (A) is seated and watching. One (B) is active and says: 'I think we need some decorations for the cake'. Then she traps her finger and play stops while she goes to wash it. Child B returns a few minutes later and continues setting the table. She comments on what she is doing. Child A is still seated but seems to be listening to the commentary.

Child A does a lot of watching in the early part of the play. She seems motivated to remain alone when B leaves and to wait for her return.

Child B's narrative on her own actions seems of interest to Child A.

Child A stands and imitates the play of Child B, laying socks on the backs of chairs. So far this is the only imitation of play to be observed. Smiles and eye contact are exchanged.

A brief relationship is formed, a connection is made. Child A endorses B's play theme through imitation. **PSE**

B goes to use the phone and then writes something on the nearby pad. A goes over and watches her. B. speaks aloud as she writes (inaudible). A watches.

Child B seems to have more ideas for how the play might progress and uses the available resources. **CLL**

1.40: B says 'I need one more thing Clare' (to A). Clare offers an object (plate) as B has just placed a plate on the table. This is accepted by B with a smile. Both sit down at the table. B is talking about having sausages for dinner and Clare responds. Brief dialogue about what they are eating.

The offering and receipt of an object generates a second shared smile.

As before, B initiates the dialogue and Child A reciprocates.

Clare (A) 'fills' a cup from the kettle on the table. The cup falls on the floor. She smiles at B who smiles back and Clare fills the cup again.

The reciprocity continues into Child A's first initiated action ('filling' the cup). **PD**

A boy (C) has entered the play area and gone to take a magazine from the magazine rack and sits and looks at it. He glances at the two girls.

KUW, CLL

A third girl enters (D), goes to the boy, takes his magazine from him, teases him by dangling it above him then gives it back with a smile when he tells her to.

This possible altercation turns into quite an extended dialogue between the boy and girl.

Clare (A) goes over to the two who are now sitting together looking at the magazine and says that it's her magazine and she 'wants it back'. Child D says 'no'. She and the boy are talking about what is in the magazine. She gives the boy another magazine and they look at it together.

Relationships are improving between C and D through shared interests. Child D is appropriately assertive. **PSE, CLL**

1.45: Child B is now tidying the table and Children A (Clare) and B seem to be playing separately within the home corner. The boy leaves the area followed by the girl who has 'teased' him (Child D).

Any previous bond between A and B does not seem strong enough to continue after Clare (Child A) has been distracted by the magazine incident.

1.50: Clare is looking at a cookery book. The boy (C) returns with Child D and makes a list of 'what we need'. A café theme is developing. Brief discussion, then boy says 'Bye bye mummy' to Child D but does not go anywhere. He is putting cups etc. on a tray and D snatches tray.
An altercation grows and the teacher intervenes to discuss and help them resolve it. Child D leaves area and boy continues alone and fetches a fork.

CLL. They go for a brief game of 'pairs' at a table but it seems they are motivated to return and continue play and a clear play theme (cafés) begins to emerge. **PSE, KUW**

However, they are not at this time able to build momentum in their play as the altercation interrupts it.

Post-observation reflections

- Rose remarked on the fruitful discussions that had come from the magazines and resolved to introduce more and to include children's comics. We also thought the children might make a TV from a cardboard box and include a TV listings magazine for the play.
- This observation took place in November; Rose felt that the children still needed time to become familiar with one another in this still relatively new classroom setting. Friendships were still forming. Children were gradually getting to know one another.
- The play themes (home play and then the beginnings of café play) were sporadically sustained and relatively brief but were both themes with which the interacting children could identify – these were *their* themes.

Scenario 2: Blue Grass Infant School

Area of Provision: Small World
Domain on the Continuum: Highly Social

Blue Grass is in an area of social priority with about 50 per cent of children receiving free school meals. It is a small nursery infant school with four teaching staff and the head and a pupil population that might range between the mid-60s to 90+ over a school year. A concern for the head, Sandra, at this time reiterates another head's concerns expressed earlier in the chapter. This was:

> the dilemma of where our five-year-olds are placed because at the moment they are between the Desirable Learning Goals and the National Curriculum. Depending on who you're speaking to, a nursery specialist will say don't do literacy and numeracy hours, others are saying five-year-olds should be doing it. This is extremely difficult; a huge pressure on very young children to be working within a framework which I don't think is suitable.

When asked what she was hoping for from participation in the research, Sandra commented:

> I think it's very good for Amy (reception teacher) to have the opportunity to mix with reception colleagues because they get very isolated. It's reassuring sometimes, teachers are self-critical and it's reassuring to hear others talk about the same issues. Also to have the chance to validate what they often can't do which is to stand back and observe. We all know we should do it, it's difficult when everything else crowds in on you, to justify setting aside half an hour and watching. This is a great opportunity for Amy to do that and learn a new technique and way of looking at play that she hasn't learned before. I don't think any of us really critically analyse what we see.

Amy, the reception teacher, had had 11 years away from teaching at one stage in her career and during this time had worked in a large inner city area with mothers and children. She had seen some of the difficulties children had experienced in becoming cooperative; indeed she had been surprised at first that they 'really didn't know how to play'. She had come to understand that some mothers and fathers had not yet come to understand the value of play and perhaps needed to play themselves before they could play with their children: 'I felt if we could give them some sense of self-worth they might see that it was valuable to play with their children'. Amy had worked in reception class for seven years.

The observation began in the Lego™ and as we see, moves into train track play. We shall see that as the play changes location, the momentum and reciprocity start to build amongst the three boys who had been observed playing together for 20 minutes by this time. They were already playing when Amy and I sat down to watch them. During post-observation reflections, we identified this play as *Highly Social* (Domain 3 on the Continuum). This observation took place in December.

2.00: Boy A shows his model and asks: 'Do you like mine?' Boy B looks but does not comment. Boy A then says: 'The windows go here'. Boy B looks and asks A: 'Where shall I put this?' (window). The dialogue turns into a more extended discussion of their models as they build.

KUW. The boys have just started to build but seem to have agreed in some way about making similar models – a vehicle of some kind. They are regularly commenting on action and showing each other their developing models. **PD**

2.05: Boy C remarks: 'Mine is going to be brilliant'. Boy A replies: 'So is mine'. A then takes a blank card from a nearby basket and a pen and says: 'These are for names'. B and C both look and a discussion begins about the size and choice of card to write on. B remarks: 'You'll have to tip it over on its side' (the card). A says: 'I can write all sorts of things so I'll write instructions shall I?' The other two reply 'yes' and he starts writing. There are discussions about how to spell words, with much helping and suggestions shared.

CLL, PSE, MD

A second common purpose has emerged – the first being the decision to make similar models. Interactions become more complex as the boys give instructions and ask/answer questions. **KUW**

2.15: They have put wheels on their models and are making play noises as they 'drive' them around the table. C remarks: 'Look at this then'. A and B look. B says 'Look at mine up there' – points to model in display area. A and C look and return to 'crashing' their cars, but carefully so they don't break.

CD

Commenting on action seems a way of connecting with peers that does not require complex discourse.

Children elsewhere in the class have spontaneously burst into song and the three boys join in and sing Christmas carols. B says: 'I'll go and get some wheels'. C says: 'Oi Daniel, I think mine looks good' and repeats it to B as he returns. Three heads come together as they discuss the model. C says: 'I'll break this off and put it here and we can pull it along' and connects his model to A's. They write more display cards: 'we're writing instructions on the inside'. One fetches his name card and asks: 'How do you do a 'n'?' His friend demonstrates.

KUW, CLL, PSE, MD

This is more than commenting on action, this is explanation and description as associated with problem setting and solving.

2.20: Boy A takes his Lego™ train to the nearby Brio™ train track, the others follow. Boy B attaches his train to A's. Boy A says: 'it fits' (the wheels are the same width as the track). They all smile: 'Look at that', 'Don't forget the back wheel', 'It has to jump over', 'It won't fit in the boat', 'It will', 'Mine's too big but yours will work', 'Quickly get yours into the boat'. The bell rings for outdoor play. They all look at the door, then at each other and smile. Play continues for several more minutes until they *have* to go outside.

The transfer to another Area of Provision seems to energize their play as they transfer resources across and see potential for further developments. Language and problem solving accelerate rapidly but are abruptly terminated by 'playtime' (a little ironic, perhaps). **KUW, MD, CD, PSE, CLL**

Post-observation reflections

- Both Amy and I felt that the play would have progressed to the Cooperative domain (the fourth and most complex domain) had it not been interrupted at such a key point by the rather ironic requirement to 'go out and play'.
- We were both impressed by the spontaneous realization, through experimentation from one child, that the wheel widths of Lego™ and Brio™ are similar. This seemed to lead to a new and creative use of the materials by the boys as they quickly transferred their play and began to build a more imaginative scenario that incorporated train track materials. They had made a connection that neither Amy nor I had made. Their use of language and problem solving grew to parallel their enthusiasm and motivation.
- The observation period prompted Amy to realize just how popular Lego™ was at that time and that perhaps the children would benefit from having more space to play with it (there were nine children around the table during the observations although we were focusing on a smaller group). She also felt it would be important to ask the boys to share their Lego™/Brio™ discovery with the class; this would value their discovery and indicate to others that they too could look for such similarities.
- Amy remarked that instruction writing had been a paired task within groups in the Literacy Hour work. It was pleasing for her to see the children incorporating this previously teacher-directed activity into their free-choice activities within the Areas of Provision.

Scenario 3: Long Deane Primary School

Area of Provision: Water
Domain on the Continuum: Cooperative

Long Deane has just over 200 children on roll. It is in a village-like environment about five miles from the city centre. It is quite close to the University which gives it a fluctuating population, usually rising by up to 30 pupils once the University term begins: 'a transient community', as Susan, the head, describes it. There are nine members of staff, two of whom job share. Susan has been in post three years. Developing the early years provision had been a priority for her on taking up the headship.

Susan describes the catchments as

> middle class, highly professional community; about 60 of our children currently come from University homes, but the vast majority from highly professional homes, it is all private housing . . . we have 17 different nationalities which is absolutely wonderful and I think brings something quite unique and special to our school.

Four and half per cent of children claim for free school meals although Susan believes that up to 13 per cent would be entitled to claim them.

When asked what she was hoping for from the research, Susan had replied:

> I would like it to impact on our learning and develop us as a school and enable us to have a superb early years department. It is also about giving teachers confidence and belief in themselves; this is not a pressurized way of developing. I think it's going to be a lovely way of enabling us to reach our goals.

Angela, the reception teacher has been at the school for 13 years and in the reception class for three years. In terms of developing the provision, she would 'like to see sand and water improved; I haven't got water at the moment but that's an area we are addressing. The role play area needs addressing and the outside play provision.' When asked what she hoped for from the research, Angela replied:

> I'm hoping to learn how to make better play provision and to observe the children. I just feel at the minute with baseline assessments that I spend most of my time with little bits, writing it down, and to focus on specific things will be good.

The observation of the water play lasted 25 minutes. The three girls played in the water throughout our observation with no other children joining the play. As we shall see, when a boy tries to join the play, it finishes abruptly. Play was already ongoing when Angela and I sat down to watch and listen. Sometimes Girls A and B played as a pair with Girl C in parallel. However, their respective play themes also combined on occasion, as the scenario shows. This interconnection of different play themes was often observed in parallel players in the research. It seemed that the longer the uninterrupted play period was, the greater the likelihood of peer recognition of the play theme being pursued and the greater the opportunities for sociability and perhaps cooperation to be nurtured.

In post-observation discussions, Angela and I agreed that the play was in the Cooperative domain on the Continuum (the fourth domain). This observation took place in March.

1.45: All three girls are scooping and pouring water. Girls A and B are also scooping small stones into their containers. Girl A says: 'Let's make that very watery' and Girl B scoops more stones into A's wide plastic basket as they discuss their activity. They both engage in silent and purposeful scooping and pouring.

Much eye contact and laughter between A and B now and throughout the play. **PSE, KUW**

Dialogue is activity-related. A shared understanding of the goal is apparent with offering and accepting of physical help. **CLL**

Girl B comments on action; she is now filling small containers with stones and discussing the imaginary contents. Alongside this, they continue to fill the larger plastic basket, reiterating 'We need more stones to make it watery'. Girl B takes stones from the small bottles to use in the plastic basket. This takes quite a long time as the bottle neck is very narrow but she perseveres for several minutes until all are out.

A new theme seems to be emerging in the paired play although neither Angela nor I know what it actually is at this point.

MD, KUW, PD

1.50: In the meantime, Girl C is in Associative Play. She occasionally watches the other two and they often glance at her. Girl C is filling small bottles with stones and arranging them on the sides of the water tray. Girl B takes a bottle from Girl C who snatches it back with a frown. B does not try again.

Is this where Girl B got her idea from (above)?

Altercation resolved quickly. **PSE**

Girls A and B are now both lining up the bottles, with stones in them, along the sides of the water tray. All three girls are playing in the same way but Girl C is still in parallel play at this point. Girl A takes a thin tube to place in a bottle and says: 'This is the clean air'. Girl B nods. Girl B talks to Girl C about the disputed bottle and they agree to place it in a certain place. Girl C places it very carefully and makes eye contact and smiles to B.

A new theme (clean air) is evident. **KUW, MD, CD**

The altercation seems forgotten and this moves Girl C into the main play theme. **PD, PSE**

2.00: It is now clear that this is a perfume shop as bottles are set out around the tray. Girl B has several times returned to the filling and emptying of small bottles with stones although it takes a long while to get the stones out. She tries several methods, shaking hard, poking her finger in and shaking, poking a tube in and shaking, banging the bottom of the bottle. Her hair band keeps falling over her face but she keeps pushing it back and carrying on, very focused, very absorbed.

There's some discussion about the shop not yet being ready to open. Girl B remarks: 'I haven't finished it yet'.

MD, PD, KUW, PSE

2.05: Girl A says: 'We need these, who needs these?' and fetches some thick pipes. It becomes an ice cream shop for a while that is serving orange juice (in the bottles). Girl B is pouring again and announces that the orange juice is now blood. Girl A resists for a while and there's some discussion, then Girl A seems to relent and is willing to take up the blood theme.

New resources seem to change the play theme, The tray seems to look 'a mess' but all three girls are discussing what the bottles and pipes are for. Girl B is negotiating a new theme that perhaps reflects her train of thought as play has developed.

Meanwhile Girl C has gone to the toilet and a boy comes to play in the water. Girls A and B tell him he cannot play (class rules state that only three are allowed in the water) as Charlotte (Girl C) is 'coming back in a minute'. He begins to cry; they *are* being forceful in their use of language. Angela intervenes and Girl A also starts to comfort him. Charlotte returns and all three girls take off their aprons and leave the boy to play.

PSE

Post-observation reflections

- Both Angela and I agreed that had we 'glanced over' at the ongoing play (rather than having observed it at some length) we might have been tempted to believe that nothing especially worthwhile was ongoing. Judging the play merely by the somewhat 'messy' appearance of the water tray at a certain point would have led to an ill-informed interpretation. Observations had revealed a period of purposeful placement of bottles as the perfume shop was established.
- Angela and I recognized that the 'shop' play theme might have already been established between the two girls (A and B) before we sat down to watch although its clarity, for us, did not emerge for some time until they used associated language to

engage with their play theme. We were made aware of our own inclinations to judge the quality of play prematurely because it didn't make 'immediate sense to us'. Understanding the play theme was essential, but sometimes it took time to become apparent.

- The re-establishing of class rules had seemed to be the initiation of the end of play for the four girls. That's not to say that they wouldn't have tried to keep the boy out had there not been a related class rule. This prompted some discussion about the 'rules of engagement' in relation to Areas of Provision. By this point, the three girls were closely focused and interconnected in their play; an 'outsider' might not have been welcome. This prompted some consideration of whether playing children might sometimes have a right to keep others out as they fear (perhaps rightly, born of previous experience) that a new player might disrupt the flow of their play themes.

- We were both intrigued at the emergence of the blood theme and the willingness of Girl A to take up this theme although it didn't seem to connect with her current interests in any especial way. We wondered if Girl A recognized its importance for Girl B because of Girl B's commitment to it. She seemed prepared to be facilitative. On the other hand, perhaps she was just enjoying the play and sensed that it might stop if she wasn't prepared to take up the theme.

Scenario 4: St Andrew's Primary School

Area of Provision: Sand
Domain on the Continuum: Cooperative

St Andrew's had almost 200 pupils in the school and the 26-place nursery class. There are nine teachers and several classroom assistants. The head, Mark, described the school: 'in terms of staffing we are quite well resourced compared to a lot of schools'. He described the catchments as 'very mixed', with 35 per cent and 43 per cent of children receiving free school meals in the previous two years. Describing the catchments in more detail, Mark went on to say:

Terraced houses, first-time owners and we also serve an estate which has areas of severe deprivation in it. Because of this, we are a social priority school. We also serve a travellers' site. Because we are close to the University, we have a large number of pupils for whom English is a second language.

The early years staff were looking at ways of bringing nursery and reception practices closer together, 'planning together as a foundation stage', although there was some frustration as government action was awaited, as Mark went on to comment:

We have kept waiting for the government to produce these documents; there's been slippage in their presentation. At the back of our minds we are slightly concerned at the nature of this material and whether it fits in with what we feel is appropriate in the Foundation Stage . . . what we want is a long-term plan so that there is a clear progression from the three-year-old to the five-year-old.

Mark identified priorities in relation to the development of the Foundation Stage, although some budget-related constraints were also recognized. However, it seems that these were not seen as insurmountable and the project involvement was already offering a rationale for moving forward:

> Another constraint is resources in terms of quality materials for the children to use . . . the materials that this project has provided, the quality of the materials is so rich that Jane [the reception teacher] has already started coming to me and saying we need more of these types of materials and where can we find the money.

When asked what he hoped for from the research, Mark replied:

> Hopefully, the discussions and the observations in all the schools will highlight ways to develop interaction skills, that people can highlight the resources that have done that particularly well.

Jane, the reception teacher, has been at St Andrew's school for eight years, working first on a temporary, part-time contract with older children – a new experience for Jane at that point – and within the past five years moving to the infant department. This was Jane's second year with reception children, although she had taught them in previous schools.

When Jane was asked to reflect on any prevailing constraints to her practice at the time of interview, she did not identify literacy or numeracy initiatives. She had already identified her 'free flow areas, where the children can select' as having the potential to promote sociability and cooperation. Jane had also identified the Areas of Provision already in the classroom: 'domestic play, role play, sand, water, there is always painting or craft, always the book corner, headphones, computer'. Her views on constraints focused on:

> the need for a quiet area that children can escape to. I would also like an outside play area. I asked Mark if we didn't have to go to Monday morning assembly, they need time just to bed down and so this term we've been trying it out and it is working well.

When asked what she was hoping for from the project, Jane replied:

> Having a better understanding of how children relate to one another. It's having the skills of knowing when to go into children's play and I think that is quite a hard thing. Nobody teaches you that at college. Sometimes you don't get it right when you go in and you question while you are sitting and joining in. I would like at the end of this six months to think, well, I have a bit more understanding, so my skills as a teacher and an educator help them move into different levels of sociability . . . I'm excited about being involved.

We watched the two boys in the sand play for 25 minutes. They had chosen two tip-up trucks, a digger, small cars and an aeroplane from the sand resources available. The observation took place in late January with both boys in their second term in the reception class. On completion of our observations, Jane and I agreed that this had been *Cooperative* Play (Domain 4 on the Continuum).

1.10: Boy A: 'I need this truck now', begins to use it. Boy B: 'I'm doing this carefully'; he is smoothing the sand and clearing a space.
Boy A: 'Now we put the truck over here', places it carefully and repeats: 'Yes, over here'.
Boy B: 'I need two things', and he collects a small car and an aeroplane to place in the line of vehicles he is making. They both make play noises and eye contact as they place vehicles in a long line on the side of the sand tray.

Their reciprocal behaviour is evident at an early stage and they take turns to comment on action and respond. This builds momentum and becomes activity-related dialogue as they line up their vehicles and move, shape and smooth the sand in the tray.
PD, MD, PSE, KUW

They discuss the road that is being made in the sand for the trucks and cars to drive along as they leave and rejoin the lined-up vehicles.
'Test it now I've made it'; 'I have to get this working'; 'Get them over here'; 'We need a bit more up here'; 'Put it up here'; 'I'm putting it up here now because I've made a place'; 'It does work'; 'We need all this up here'.

There is a continuous stream of dialogue as they clear and smooth sand, move vehicles in and out of the line. They both seem clear about the goals and purposes of the play.
CLL, CD

In the middle of this dialogue, Boy B remarks while making very 'firm' eye contact: 'We share these don't we?', referring it seems to the trucks and the digger (there are two trucks but only one digger).

Play rules are being established in an appropriately assertive way.
PSE, CLL

1.20: They are building a ramp up to the ledge where they are lining up the vehicles. They clear together and move the sand around using the digger. Boy A says it's his turn to have the digger.

A dramatic scenario is being enacted through their reciprocal actions.
CD, KUW, CLL

Boy B continues for a while and then passes it over saying, 'It's your turn now but it's my turn again soon, isn't it?' Boy A nods and begins to use the digger. Boy B smoothes the sand and shapes the ramp. He says 'You need the same as me' and searches in the sand for another plane but cannot find one.

Boy B seems to introduce many of the new ideas – lining up the vehicles, the ramp, burying vehicles – but Boy A seems happy to follow these themes.

1.25: Boy B asks: 'Are we doing all this stuff or not?' and Boy A says 'Yes'. Boy B says: 'Come on' and seems to work faster: 'We need to get through this bit'. Boy A: 'I have to bury one of mine' and buries a car in the sand. Boy A says: 'This is your digger but I'm using it'.

The first question seems to be directed at bringing Boy A back into the flow of the play, he is deeply absorbed in shifting sand with the digger. Perhaps Boy A senses Boy B may take the digger back if he is not physically attached to it, so signals continued use. **PSE**

Boy A watches Boy B filling the trucks and moving sand around and remarks: 'I see what you mean'. Boy B asks: 'Is it my turn to have the digger?' and Boy A drives it to him, saying: 'We share don't we?' The play continues in the same way until they both brush the sand from their hands and decide to go and play elsewhere.

It's not clear whether this is a question or an affirmation.

Post-observation reflections

- The levels of negotiation and problem solving that were used to fairly distribute the use of the one digger were impressive. Jane had thought at one point that she should have made two diggers available as there were two large trucks. On reflection she felt that having only one was beneficial and had been pleased to hear the boys talking about sharing as this is something she has been emphasizing with the children at circle time discussions.
- One boy in particular (Boy B) seemed to lead the play. Jane said this was characteristic of him. He had many ideas when playing in other Areas of Provision and he had a way of sharing those ideas that prompted other children to follow his lead. He was skilful at explaining what he was doing and this commentary seemed to help other children recognize the play theme that was being enacted.
- Jane had felt that the quality and consistency of the sand supported their need to mould the sand; dry sand would not have allowed them to do this and it was a very important part of this activity.
- Although these two boys did not do so, Jane said she encouraged children to fetch resources from other areas in the room to combine with whatever they were playing with. She wondered if small world figures might have extended the play further

had the boys gone to find them. However, she also acknowledged that the boys may not have been interested in figures at this point, but in design and vehicle movement.

Scenario 5: Royal Whittington Primary School

Area of Provision: Large Construction
Domain: Cooperative

Royal Whittington is a large primary school with just over 450 pupils at the time of the research, having grown quite substantially during the previous two years because of new housing developments. The school has 19 teachers, with two full-time teachers and a teacher support in the reception class base and plans for a third teacher to be appointed the following term. Although only a relatively small number of pupils received free meals (4.6 per cent) there were other characteristics of the school population that, in the words of Paul, the head, 'created pockets of difficulty'. Because of local circumstances there was 'quite a lot of pupil movement' as many families stayed in the area for a relatively short term. In the year prior to the research taking place, for example, between 8 per cent and 15 per cent of new children had transferred into different year groups across the school.

Paul had been in post for two years. In terms of recent difficulties, Paul identified, as others heads had done, that:

> The reception teachers found it difficult, when we were doing the literacy strategy training, and the numeracy, that they're not totally sure how it relates to them. They've had mixed messages from training courses. I felt last year there was a conflict between trying to work towards Desirable Outcomes and trying to take on board bits of the literacy strategy. They fell between two stools . . . trying to do the literacy was working against social development and the opportunity for children to make choices.

When asked what he hoped for from involvement in the project, Paul had replied:

> I hope that both I and the reception teachers will gain a clearer idea of what we really want to develop. Often, when you're looking at something and you're focused and detailed, it does help to give a clearer understanding . . . play in the widest sense, so often, people see things like lack of resources, lack of space, lack of this, lack of that as being issues that prevent it rather than seeing how they can facilitate it.

There were two reception teachers at this point in Royal Whittington School, and both were interviewed. June had worked there for 12 years and this was her sixth year in the reception class. Some recent courses had helped reiterate the value of play for this age group: 'different ways of getting literacy into play, incorporate writing skills in the role play area that I hadn't thought of before'. The course had encouraged the reception staff to set up Areas of Provision, although June felt that 'we are still consolidating on that'.

When asked what she hoped for from involvement in the research, June had replied:

> I want to improve my understanding of how they are developing through play but I also want to improve my skills of observing.

Catherine, the second of the two reception teachers, had been at Royal Whittington School for 18 years: 'I'm probably the longest standing teacher here'. This was her third period of working with the reception age group at the school. She recognized that Paul had brought a proactive approach to supporting developments in the early years of the school. He had invited the early years adviser into school to support developments and had maintained contact with her when she had left the authority to work for an early years consultancy. Both June and Catherine maintained that this advice had been strong and very positive in helping them develop their provision over a period of time. They saw their involvement in the research as a continuation of this period of development for them.

The following scenario is from a paired observation with Catherine.

Catherine and I observed the large construction play for 25 minutes. The children had differently sized wooden blocks. Someone had brought Mobilo™ into the area. The observations show same-gender play at the outset. This developed to boy/girl play and Catherine and I decided that overall, this play was in the *Cooperative domain* on the Continuum between the three players who become most closely involved with one another. The observation took place in February.

1.25: Two girls and two boys are playing as we sit to observe. Boy A says to Boy B: 'Hey, look'. Boy B looks at Boy A's design and smiles. Boy A asks: 'Shall we make a helicopter?' Boy B says 'Yes,' and moves closer. They are playing with the Mobilo™.	Eye contact and smiles plus instruction and positive response create an opportunity for closer proximity and socialization begins between the two boys. **CLL, PSE**
Girl A remarks: 'I'm trying to make a house'. She is locating bricks on the floor. Girl B looks over and then leaves the area.	Girl A's comment on action invites a look from Girl B but it does not progress further at this point.
1.30: Boy A calls to Boy B: 'Look at my helicopter'. Boy B looks and nods and smiles. Boy A begins to build a tower and calls to Boy B: 'Look at this'. Boy B nods and says: 'Very nice'.	Boy A is persistent in his social invitations. Boy B is responsive but has not yet taken the initiative to connect fully with the play. **CLL**

The tower starts to wobble. Girl A goes across and holds the design for Boy A. She kneels to keep it stable while he adds bricks. It falls and they laugh and begin to build it again. Boy B comes across to watch and then begins to help. Girl A goes back to her floor design and Boy A follows her. Boy B continues with the tower design but looks over at them as Boy A adds bricks to the girl's design.

Girl A points out where his design is weak: 'it's too thin'.

CLL, MD, KUW, CD, PSE

Boy B seems to want to connect with Boy A.

1.35: Boy A and Girl A begin a second layer on the floor-based design. Girl A remarks: 'We'll make it go in and out' and Boy A nods and continues to get and place bricks. Girl A says to Boy B, who is watching: 'This is the queen's house and you can be the king'. He continues to build his own design slightly apart from the boy and girl. Boy A accidentally backs into Boy B's design and a little bit falls. Eye contact and Boy B laughs after Boy A laughs. Girl A smiles and takes a brick from Boy B's design for her own. Boy B says: 'I'm making it bigger than yours'. Boy A remarks to girl: 'We don't care, do we?'

MD, KUW, CD

Perhaps a play theme is emerging.

Bricks are becoming in short supply. The 'palace' theme seems to becoming well-established as the building grows in size.

Boy C enters the play area and watches. Girl A says: 'What shall we do here?' Boy C replies: 'Put these in here' and gives her two bricks. Girl A takes them and smiles.

Boy C seems to have negotiated a successful entry by offering Girl A what she needs – more bricks. **PSE**

Activity-related dialogue continues for some time between the two players. Explanations and descriptions are used. Momentum builds in the play. **CLL, CD, PD, MD**

1.45: Boy B comes over and asks for another brick and Girl A gives him one and smiles at him. Boy A asks him: 'What are you making?' His reply is inaudible.

Object requested and given. Boy B never becomes Highly Social but he does connect in small ways with other players. **PSE**

| Boy C and Boy A are playing together on the floor. Girl A is making 'a road for the cars'. The two boys have developed a fire theme in their play. Play continues until tidy-up time. | Offering and accepting of physical help continues. The three players seem to share common goals. |

Post-observation reflections

- Girl A seems to have driven the play overall, although not in any overt or directive way. Her design (floor-based) was far more stable than Boy A's tower design and she introduced the palace theme, which seemed readily accepted by the other male players.
- Boy B was new to the reception class and perhaps was still 'finding his way' amongst new friends. Despite the very slight altercation, their play was amicable and he seemed to enjoy and perhaps benefit from the occasional interactions and the chance to watch the play as the theme of 'palaces' developed over time.
- The other players were more familiar with one another. It was interesting to note how Boy C had used the offering of objects to gain successful entry to the play. Observations have shown that children who watch and gain a feel for the ongoing theme and who then offer an object or a suggestion that is related, generally have more success in being accepted. We wondered if this was a skill that children come to intuitively and whether or not all children actually come to it. Could it, we wondered, be modelled for children by adult players?
- The children had brought the Mobilo™ into the area, and Catherine was pleased that they felt able to manage their environment in this way. We recognized that talking to children about how they used resources might encourage them to continue combining different resources; this does seem to have to be made explicit for them amid rules about classroom behaviour.

Some emerging principles to underpin Areas of Provision

Allowing children the time to sustain and develop their play

As observations progressed, we all began to recognize how some aspects of classroom life might prematurely end ongoing play that was already, or that had the potential to become, highly sociable and cooperative. It was possible to recognize increased reciprocity between players as it built and alongside this, to see how momentum could grow as interactions became theme-related and the themes became commonly understood and accepted by players. This is quite a difficult quality to convey in the scenarios because we only have a limited amount of detail in the observational notes that were made. The Highly Social play of the Brio™ and Lego™ might have continued to become Cooperative had playtime not interrupted it; the burst of reciprocity and complex language use that accompanied the 'discovery' about wheel widths would probably have continued.

We saw in the water play how the application of classroom rules (only three allowed in the water) took the girls away from their play to 'deal with' the approaching boy and how this subsequently ended the play for them. The boy may have felt that his approach was legitimate, as one girl was absent from play. Mention was also made of the girls' desire to protect their play from a seemingly insensitive outsider. In their case the class rules might have been very useful to them. Throughout the observations, the teachers and I often reflected on the often present rule concerning the numbers of children 'allowed' in certain Areas of Provision. There were several instances of rule application disrupting play *and* prompting teacher intervention. Teachers experimented with rule removal and found, from observations, that children often regulated themselves. If an area is too full, it is inevitably less satisfying for a child because resources are limited. Rather than leading to more altercations, the observations showed that children often watched but did not always join in such cases, perhaps deciding to return at another time. The teachers felt that because they were becoming committed to making all Areas of Provision available on a regular basis to the children (although not necessarily all of them simultaneously), the children seemed less anxious about 'getting their go' regardless of numbers and access and were prepared to wait for another time. Removing rules about access did not lead to anarchy and allowed playing children to continue playing for longer periods because teachers ceased applying the 'coming out because you've been in long enough' rule.

High levels of reciprocity among interacting players sustained the momentum of the play and, with it, engaged the children's commitment to the exploration and development of the play theme. This in turn led to greater complexity of language use and ideas, particularly when leaders emerged whose ideas and experiences were incorporated into the play in ways that participating players could recognize as familiar and accessible. Observing the play helped us to better understand the reality of this process. Thinking about the water play and the sand play, both these scenarios might have looked 'messy' (the bottles in the water tray) or repetitive (the shifting and piling of sand) from a distance or if only subjected to an occasional glance by an adult. Listening and watching had given the play much greater meaning. It had also allowed access to the nuances of relationship building, the willingness to take turns in the sand, the coming together of associative players in the water, as well as allowing the watching adults some insights into the preoccupations and interests of children. This, in turn, gives children's preoccupations and personal interests greater status in the adults' eyes and also encourages adults to think about how they might begin to structure, extend and organize the Areas of Provision to maximize the contribution of play to children's learning and understanding.

Recognizing and nurturing play themes

In relation to the water play, comment was made about how long it took to recognize that this was a perfume shop. The children had 'signed up' to the theme before Angela and I began to watch the three girls. Where the players could take meaning from the placing of bottles, the need for stones in the bottles, the need to make it 'watery' and the function of the pipe for 'clean air', this was meaningless for a relatively long period to us as we watched. This was an observational phenomenon which we each came to recognize and learned to be patient about. However, in the absence of such under-standing it is quite difficult to engage intellectually with the play. It can bring a quality of 'boredom' to the observations. Humans need to understand in order to engage intellectually. When we lack understanding, we tend to disengage and there is a real temptation to ascribe low status to an activity that appears meaningless. We learned that this is a real danger in relation to the interpretation and understanding of children's play. If we do not watch for a sufficient time so as to recognize the unifying theme(s) that the children have ascribed to their play, or to see the theme change and develop, then there can be tendency to dismiss the play as 'low level', 'stereotypical' or 'unchallenging'.

We can also begin to see from the above scenarios how the well-established play themes are linked to the greater potential for play to progress from the Associative domain through the Social to the Highly Social and Cooperative domains.

In the home corner, the play themes seemed transient and single-purpose. Girl A copies Girl B in laying socks on chairs; she offers a plate to B as she lays the table. Girl B may have had a party theme in mind. She had mentioned needing decorations for a cake but then had trapped her finger and did not mention parties on her return. This is not to say that such a theme wasn't clear in her mind but later, their brief dialogue is about having sausages for dinner. They are connecting but, as noted above, the entry of other players seems to disturb this connection; it seems too fragile to withstand this disruption.

In the Lego®, the decision to make similar models connects the three boys in their play. They have a shared goal, commonly understood and elaborated through the giving and taking of instructions and through asking and answering questions. This articulation of a shared goal or goals seems important in building sociability and leading on to cooperation because it sustains the momentum of the play by nurturing recipro-city, something that seemed only brief in the home corner play. In the Lego® play, the shared goals are linked to problem solving and we see them further expand when the transfer to the Brio® train track is made. Boy A's idea and investigation of the idea made this possible and their collective engagement with the train track and their models took them into a problem solving scenario concerned with transportation.

Moving finally to the large construction play, we see the helicopter theme briefly connecting the two boys, then one moving to the bricks. The helicopter builder tries to sustain his peers' interest but later is tempted to join in the construction of the tower. Girl A progresses from her 'house' and Boy A is tempted to join her, leaving the 'tower' to Boy B (who is new to the class) for the 'queen's house'. When Boy C comes along, he and Boy A introduce a fire theme to the queen's house which seems acceptable, prompting Girl A to make some roads for the cars.

Engaging with a play theme gives the children a common purpose. These themes are drawn from their knowledge of and experiences in the world. Common purpose can lead them to sociability and cooperation. Cooperation requires a shared understanding of goals and associated problem setting and solving in their achievement. When children are cooperating their language becomes richer, their motivation for continued engage-ment seems greater, the levels of reciprocity seem higher and all of these seem to create and sustain a momentum that continually engages them one with the other and with the problem setting and solving.

Fostering friendships for young children

We need to be aware of just how well the children might know one another as we watch them playing alongside and together. Familiarity and friendship are no less key factors in their lives than they might be in the lives of adults. Because children find themselves in rooms together, it does not necessarily follow that they will become friends each in the same way. Children may be drawn to some peers more readily than others. Having said this, the teachers often remarked on being surprised at seeing some children playing together – often children whom they had not associated as 'being friends' until the observations, seemingly, revealed otherwise. This might suggest some degree of pragmatism and flexibility in the ways in which young children develop friendships in early years settings as they become more confident in this initially unfamiliar environment. It might also suggest that children can be attracted by ongoing play situations rather than by actual players but that some degree of familiarity will facilitate both their desire to enter ongoing play and the likelihood of being accepted by already interacting peers.

These scenarios have also drawn attention to the ways in which children sometimes actively seek to keep their peers out of the play, and have prompted some consideration of whether this might be legitimate at times. In both the home corner and the water play, we saw attempts to make entering children feel unwelcome. In the home corner Clare tries to assert her right to the magazine that the new boy has taken up (although he isn't seeking any direct impact on her ongoing activity). In the water, the girls are quite forceful with the new boy. In both cases, their desire to be 'territorial' may stem from a desire to protect their play from potential disruption by newcomers who seemingly demonstrate little or no sensitivity to it. In contrast, in the large construction play, we see an entering boy quickly assimilated because he offers bricks to the girl building, demonstrating a clear understanding of purpose and a willingness to conform and participate.

Helping behaviours are important in sustaining play and in leading towards co-operative play. The entering boy was helpful, as was Girl A in the large construction area, holding the wobbly tower. Each was rewarded, the boy by being allowed entry and the girl, perhaps, by being supported in the development of the 'her' palace theme by the boys. In the sand, the helping and turn-taking lasted throughout as the two boys shared the single digger and sustained their 'design and digging' theme for a long period.

Opportunities to explain, describe and instruct also lead into cooperative play. We saw in the Lego® play how the momentum grew between the three boys once they transferred their Lego® to the Brio® train track. This intellectual connection was the basis for renewed vigour in the play. Their smile of complicity and understanding when the 'playtime' bell rang suggested heightened understanding across all three players that their play could continue almost in defiance of understood convention. The bond of friendship seemed very strong in their unspoken complicity.

Linking in with the Foundation Stage Curriculum

A trawl through the five scenarios illustrates how each of them has substantial potential for addressing the six Areas of Learning within the Foundation Stage Curriculum. It is hoped that this will reassure practitioners that Areas of Provision can legitimately and creatively assist them in achieving these educational goals for young children but that alongside this, they can provide so much more.

The intention in the following chapters is to continue to offer scenarios and associated reflection from the observed play to support these claims. First of all, however, it seems timely to introduce the Social Play Continuum in greater detail.

Chapter 2

The Social Play Continuum

The word 'continuum' is defined in the dictionary as: 'a continuous series or whole, no part of which is perceptibly different from the adjacent parts'. Strictly speaking, this is not a definition that accurately describes the Social Play Continuum, as this continuum is designed to depict increasing complexity in language and behaviour through four adjacent categories of sociability. As a result, there *are* perceptible changes in the adjacent categories or 'domains' as these behaviours and language progress towards the Cooperative domain.

Just to recap, there are four domains or adjacent parts of the Continuum – Associative, Social, Highly Social, and Cooperative. The decision to retain the descriptor 'Continuum' reflects that strong dimension of continuity that is implicit in the dictionary definition of the word. It is perhaps also important to restate a point made in the Introduction in that the Continuum, although comprehensive, remains incomplete. The research has identified progression through the study of three- to six-year-olds so far. There are certainly further developments to be made in it through the study of younger and older children. But for now, the word 'Continuum' conveys the strong sense of continuity and progression in the play that I hope this tool conveys to those who choose to use it to support their observations. The Continuum has been designed, tested and refined over many years of observations in nursery, reception and Year 1 settings. Some of this development work has been discussed elsewhere (Broadhead, 1997, 2001). Teacher evaluations have led to alterations in the content and the layout of the Continuum to arrive at its present form.

This chapter presents and describes the Continuum in some detail as a prelude to Chapter 3, which offers further guidance on making observations in early years settings. It is Chapter 3 that looks more closely at the need for and purposes of observation and which also acknowledges that making time to observe play, and taking real meaning from those observations and interpretations, is not unproblematic for practitioners. Educators have a natural desire to be 'active' within the learning process. Observation may seem, on the surface, to be a relatively passive activity.

However, observation is an intellectually challenging and demanding task, requiring concentration and reflection if truly informed interpretations of play are to be made. It is a skill-based activity as well as an intellectual activity and, like all skills, benefits from practice. This chapter opens with a look at a small part of what we know about the growth of sociability in young children. It goes on to describe the Continuum in detail and, in conclusion, offers some evaluative comments about the use of the Continuum and about observing children's play, from teachers involved in the ongoing research.

Becoming sociable and cooperative

Face-to-face interactions are among our earliest experiences of social interaction. From two months onwards this is a primary means of socializing and, as visual efficiency improves, this mode of interaction provokes responses and then initiation by the young infant (Schaffer, 1996). From about five months of age, the emergence of manipulative abilities allows the young infant to examine and explore objects and these objects become an increasingly important part of the baby's social interactions with familiar adults as maturation occurs (Kaye and Fogel, 1980). There is no doubt that the very young infant is totally dependent on the willingness of those around her/him to initiate and sustain their socializing opportunities, but these 'self-regulating others and personified things indicate the degree to which the subjective world of infants is deeply social' (Stern, 1998:123).

Stern argues that infants are already experiencing a sense of their core self and are bringing this sense of self-being to their social experiences with others. He argues that these forms of 'being with' are active constructions by the young child. This sense of self grows out of regular contact with a significant other person or persons. This sense of self and other are fused initially but, over time, the sense of self becomes distinguished and differentiated (Main et al., 1985). There is some support for the view that securely attached infants develop their self-concept faster than insecurely attached infants (Schneider-Rosen and Cicchetti, 1984; Pipp et al., 1993). From these earliest months, the interconnections between the growth of concepts that begin to shape our knowledge and understanding of the world, the emergence of self-identity and opportunities for socialization are a fundamental yet essential part of the child's natural development.

Shared frameworks of meaning become increasingly important, Stern (1998) argues, as the child's theory of mind begins to develop from seven to nine months onwards. Realization grows and the infant gradually begins to recognize that inner (subjective) experiences can be shared with those familiar to us. Over the following months and into the second year of life, the young child increasingly recognizes their own capacity to initiate, share, demand and reject. The young child comes to recognize that their actions provoke responsive actions and that they can have some control, through their initiated actions, over the directions that these interactions might take. They begin to shape their social experiences more actively, sometimes to prolong them when others might want to end them and to initiate them more easily when they want to play with others. Physical mobility rapidly expands their universe and the 'personified things' of the relatively immobilized infant give way to the persistent exploration and investigation of a world of exciting (and sometimes dangerous) objects to stimulate and engage.

The rapid development of language from the second year of life and beyond brings an important dimension to the connections between conceptual growth, self-identity and socialization. Not only does their sense of self acquire new attributes, but here is a new medium through which self and others create and share new meanings (Stern, 1998). During this period, emotional expression expands. Pride and shame may appear by the end of the second year as the young child learns to self-evaluate. Joy and anger will usually (and often) be extremely expressed before self-control can begin to emerge. Self-control takes time to develop, tantrums may be commonplace and regulation can only emerge through socialization processes that help the child to see greater benefits from being in control rather than out of control (Chorpita and Barlow, 1998). While the sense of self might sometimes scream for satisfaction and gratification, signs of helping, caring, sharing and sympathy are also evident in this second year (Rhinegold, 1982; Zahn-Waxler *et al.*, 1992; Hay, 1994). Children are capable of such pro-social behaviours at an early age and a key question for adults is, under what kinds of conditions and in what kinds of circumstances are young children most likely to act in pro-social ways with their peers?

As children move from family-based settings into the wider world of pre-school and childcare, their relatively unlimited access to a key adult changes. Depending on their age and the setting, they will be sharing adults with other children to some degree. Dowling (2000) equates it with an adult starting a new job, but the child has far less experience of life on which to draw. This move to a group is momentous and will impact, for better or worse, on the child's self-concept and self-esteem. However, the growing child's capacity for interacting with more than one person simultaneously has already started to develop by age three, more especially when the child is in a secure and familiar environment with adults and children s/he has come to know.

Rapidly growing language skills, increasing self-control, desires for autonomy, inde-pendence and knowledge can each assist the child in their participation in and active contribution to a more complex and demanding social environment. However, there are still a considerable number of skills to be developed and steps to be taken to be suc-cessful in this new world. The growth of self in relation to a limited number of 'others' needs expansion as those, now multiple 'others' also exert their desires and interests simultaneously with one's own. The growing child must learn to compromise if s/he is to engage with others, one of the earliest forms of which is turn-taking. Here, the child delays instant gratification because s/he comes to understand how the wait, usually in the company of others, can be exciting and socially meaningful. Anticipation becomes a time for reflection as well as interaction. Plans are made, decisions are taken. Conscious thought begins to have impact on subsequent action. Friendships begin to be formed and early friendships are an important part of social understanding and communicative intelligence (Faulkner and Miell, 1993).

The Social Play Continuum has documented the language and action of interacting peers through observations of children from age three to six years. How do children use language and action to shape and manage their interactions with their peers? Having gained this information, how might it be presented so as to illustrate the increasingly complex ways in which children are able to operate – given the right conditions of course – socially and cooperatively?

Let us move on to look at Side 1 of the Social Play Continuum, section by section (see Table 2.1).

Table 2.1 The Social Play Continuum – Side 1: a tool for play observation, pupil assessment and evaluation of Areas of Provision

| Observation start time: | Children entering play: | Observation finish time: |
| Area of provision: | Children leaving play: | |

L = Language   A = Action observed   L/A = Language and Action combined
RL = Reciprocal language   RA = Reciprocal Action   RL/RA = Reciprocal language and reciprocal action combined

ASSOCIATIVE DOMAIN	SOCIAL DOMAIN	HIGHLY SOCIAL DOMAIN	COOPERATIVE DOMAIN
A: Looks towards peers	A: Smiling	RA: Offering/accepting of objects evident	RA: Offering/accepting objects sustains/extends play theme
A: Watches play	A: Laughter	RL: Dialogue, a mix of activity related and non-related but a play theme is evident	RL: Sustained dialogue is activity related and clear theme(s) emerge
A: Imitates play	L: Play noises, play voice		
A/L: Object offered, not accepted	RA: Eye contact made	RL: Comment on own action/ described intent with acknowledgement leading to extended exchange	RL: Explanations/descriptions utilized
A/L: Object taken, altercation	A: Object taken, no altercation		RL/RA: New ideas/resources extends play and is sustained
A: Parallel play period	RA: Object offered and received	RL: Sporadic dialogue develops role play themes	RL/RA: Children display a shared understanding of goals
L: Self-talk	L/A: Consent sought and object accessed	RA/L: Eye contact/laughter (play noise) combined as behavioural cluster	RL: Offering and accepting verbal help
A/L: Comment on action directed at peer; peer does not respond	L: Approval sought, not given		
	RL: Approval sought and given	RA/RL: Brief reciprocal sequence e.g. giving/following instructions seeking/giving approval, offering, accepting objects, asking/ answering questions	
	L: Instruction given, no response		
	L/RA: Instruction given, positive response	RL/RA: New ideas or resources have impact on developing theme	
	L: Question asked, no response		
	RL: Question asked, response given		
	L/RA: Comment on own action/ described intent directed at peer, peer looks		
	RL: Comment on own action/ described intent directed at peer, verbal response		

Emergent play themes noted:

© RoutledgeFalmer (2003)

42   The Social Play Contin

The headings

The Social P
evaluation

Si

nd footing of the Continuum

lay Continuum is a tool for play observation, pupil assessment and of Areas of Provision.

e I of the Continuum

Observation start time:

Children entering play:

Area of Provision:

Children leaving play:

Observation finish time:

L = *Language* **A** = *Action observed* **L/A** = *Language and Action combined*

RL = *Reciprocal language* **RA** = *Reciprocal action* **RL/RA** = *Reciprocal language and reciprocal action combined*

Noting the observation start and finish times allows the observer to do two things:

(a) to identify the length of time that the observation lasted when looking at the observational recording at a later date
(b) to be systematic where necessary in ensuring that equal times are being given to different Areas of Provision if comparisons are to be made.

Similarly, in noting the Area of Provision in focus, the record of the observation offers useful detail at a later reference point. Although it is really helpful to an observer if s/he can discuss the observations with a paired observer directly afterwards, that is not always possible so sufficient detail is needed to assist recall, either for self-reflection or for joint reflections at a later point with a colleague or with a parent. Also, if a practitioner wishes to use the Continuum for personal research, the necessary detail will add validity to the later analysis of all the research data (these ideas are explored more fully in Chapter 3).

Similarly, it is useful in aiding later reflections to know who enters and leaves the play. When the children are known to the observer, this can be done with the use of initials. Where the observer does not know the children, this can be B (boy) or G (girl).

The coding system (**L**, **A**, etc.) is explained on the sheet as the letter abbreviations are used, as shorthand in each of the domains. The observer is asked to do four things:

(a) to distinguish between language and action during the observation
(b) to note where language and action begin to combine in children's interactions
(c) to recognize where language and action become reciprocal, i.e. where one child's initiated language or action receives a response of some kind from a peer

(d) to recognize the high levels of complexity being sustained by playing children when reciprocated language and reciprocated action combine as in the Cooperative domain.

In brief, the observer is asked to note, perhaps with a tick, each observed behaviour or use of language during the observation period. To do this, the observer needs to become familiar with the Continuum. Observer activity is discussed more fully in Chapter 3 but to aid familiarity, each domain is now discussed in some detail.

At the bottom of Side 1 of the Continuum is a small space for the observer to note the *emergent play themes*. As the scenarios in Chapter 1 have shown, it is important in understanding the purpose of the play to be aware of how the children are directing the play if and when it has a clear theme. In Associative and Social play, the theme may belong to one child rather than be shared, or may be briefly shared by a pair of children. This should still be noted, as emergent themes are as important in understanding play in the Social domain as are the more established and prolonged themes of Highly Social and Cooperative play. In general, when themes become more widely shared, or begin to extend within the play, the play begins to enter the Highly Social domain. It is recognition of the theme that also enables the observer to see the connections that children might be making between adult-directed activities and their own, free choice activities.

The Associative domain explained

ASSOCIATIVE DOMAIN

A: Looks towards peers

A: Watches play

A: Imitates play

A: Object offered, not accepted

A/L: Object taken, altercation

A: Parallel play period

- In this domain, we can see that the play is for the most part in parallel to peers. The main behaviours are action-based. Watching and imitation may be relatively frequent as shared frameworks of meaning are developing as children play in an Area of Provision.

- Object play is important in this domain, as it has been for the developing infant; the offering of an object becomes the first recognizable attempt at reciprocity but in this domain it may be ignored or an object may be taken from a parallel player and followed by altercation.

continued on next page

L: Self-talk

- Self-talk is recognized as Vygotsky described it (as an indicator of 'thinking out loud') rather than as Piaget described it (as a sign of egocentrism). Even as adults we may self-talk when confronted with a problem.

A/L: Comment on action directed at peer;
peer does not respond

- Comment on action is slightly different from self-talk in that it is not an introspective reflection; rather, the head may be lifted or the gaze directed as the child says 'I'm putting the car in the garage' as almost an invitation to play. When directed at a peer, as a comment, or even if the voice lifts a little to carry further, it invites reciprocity. As with object offering, this denotes initial attempts to build reciprocity.

The Social domain explained

SOCIAL DOMAIN

A: Smiling

A: Laughter

L: Play noises, play voice

RA: Eye contact made

A: Object taken, no altercation

RA: Object offered and received

L/A: Consent sought and object accessed

L: Approval sought, not given

RL: Approval sought and given

L: Instruction given, no response

- The face remains important for its key signals, and smiling and laughter are now in evidence, sometimes to self and sometimes to others. Similarly with play noises, these may be to self or in conjunction with others. The play noise is a clearer invitation to respond than was the self-talk of the Associative domain because it is often more vigorous, designed to attract attention. It is similar in type to 'comments on action'.

- In this domain, we can see that the reciprocity (**R**) is growing. Eye contact (so important to the developing baby) is still in evidence but is now being given *and* returned. Objects that are offered are accepted and this action is often accompanied by eye contact as interacting peers more frequently register faces and responses. Sometimes, an object is still taken without permission but this is not followed by altercation as compromise takes its place.

continued on next page

L/RA: Instruction given, positive response

L: Question asked, no response

RL: Question asked, response given

L/RA: Comment on own action/described intent directed at peer, peer looks

RL: Comment on own action/ described intent directed at peer, verbal response

- Language is being used in more complex ways in the Social domain, to seek approval: 'My house has got two doors, isn't it good?'; to give instructions: 'Hold this while I pour water in'; and to ask questions: 'Shall we make this bigger?' Peers may or may not respond. These tend to be relatively isolated and sporadic interactions in this domain.

- It may not be easy for the observer to detect any significant differences between a child seeking approval and a child commenting on their own action or describing intent. It's a matter of interpretation. When trialling the materials, it was decided that it was important to retain the distinct categories. As observational skills developed with time and practice, the capacity to make distinctions also developed. It was felt to be important to be as precise as possible in describing children's behaviour and interactions.

The Highly Social domain explained

HIGHLY SOCIAL DOMAIN

RA: Offering/accepting of objects evident

RL: Dialogue a mix of activity related and non-related but a theme is evident

RL: Comment on own action/ described intent with acknowledgement leading to extended exchange

RL: Sporadic dialogue develops role play themes

- The offering and accepting of objects is becoming more integrated into the flow of the play but remains important in making and sustaining social connections.

- In this domain, it becomes apparent that the levels of reciprocity in the play are increasing. As a result, the play is gaining momentum as the exchanges between playing peers become longer.

continued on next page

RA/L: Eye contact/laughter, (play noise) combined as behavioural cluster

- Eye contact and facial expressions remain important but children are now taking the signals for reciprocity from language and action and relying less on facial expressions for sustaining links with peers.

RA/RL: Brief reciprocal sequences, e.g. giving/following instructions, seeking/giving approval, offering/accepting objects, asking/answering questions

- These more extended exchanges allow children to communicate and develop their play themes. But, as noted previously, observers must beware. Sometimes children establish a theme before the observer arrives and have no need to reiterate it. This aspect is discussed in the next chapter.

RL/RA: New ideas or resources have some impact on the developing theme

- When there is a shared understanding of the play theme, children can begin to incorporate their own experiences, ideas and the available resources into the play. Chapter 4 looks at this aspect in more detail.

The Cooperative domain explained

COOPERATIVE DOMAIN

RA: Offering/accepting objects sustains/extends play theme

- In this domain, the main purpose for the offering and accepting of objects is to develop the clear play themes children are engaging with. The objects become incidental to relationship building and integral to problem-solving activities and goal achievement.

RL: Sustained dialogue is activity-related and clear theme(s) emerge

- The momentum is such that just about all the dialogue is activity-related but not necessarily frequent. The children become immersed in their play, wholly absorbed and engaged; all that they say and do is an expression of their united engagement with the play theme and the attainment of their goals.

continued on next page

RL: Explanations/descriptions utilized

- Children no longer comment on action and seldom make play noises but explain and describe to peers what they are doing and why.

RL/RA: New ideas/resources extend play and are sustained

RL/RA: Children display a shared understanding of goals

- Children seek out and incorporate resources from wherever they can to extend and expand the play themes; the resources are an important part of how they can bring their ideas and experiences to life.

RL: Offering and accepting of verbal help

RA: Offering and accepting of physical help

- In seeking to achieve their goals, children recognize times when peers need help and begin to respond verbally with suggestions and physically with assistance.

RL/RA: Verbal and physical help combined

RL/RA: Problem identified and solved

RL/RA: Sustained dramatic scenarios enacted linked to play theme(s)

- The role play begins to take on clear dramatic qualities. Children remain in character for longer periods, also interacting in character for extended periods. Scenarios emerge; characters make entrances and exits in more formalized ways. Children only 'break out' of character to negotiate and agree plot development or the integration of new characters. Close observation reveals that what at first may seem like parallel play is often the development of a character, in character. Some of these scenarios are illustrated in Chapter 4.

Side 2 of the Continuum: reflecting on and categorizing the observed play

Having observed the children at play in a selected Area of Provision, and having noted on the observational schedule every instance of language and action and reciprocity, the observer is then asked to make a judgement as to which of the domains they feel best represents the observed play, overall (see Table 2.2). Side 2 of the Social Play Continuum is designed to support this reflection. This time of reflection (and it may only need a few minutes) is not only about categorizing the play, however.

It is at this point that the practitioner can most effectively and simultaneously engage with:

1   ideas and possibilities for improving the Area of Provision in focus
2   Foundation Stage Profiling activity relating to individual children

Table 2.2 The Social Play Continuum – Side 2: reflecting on and categorizing observed play

Increasing levels of reciprocity and momentum

Characteristics of associative play	Characteristics of social play	Characteristics of highly social play	Characteristics of cooperative play
Self-talk does not elicit a response No/very little dialogue No/very little eye contact Seemingly little regard for proximity of peers Limited periods of peer interaction Overtures ignored	May involve much movement indoors or outdoors Children leave and join the play at frequent intervals Associative players often nearby Little development of play ideas, often repetitive Little shared understanding of goal achievement Dialogue does not always relate to activity Play punctuated by periods of associative play Altercations evident when play returns to associative Adult intervention may often be sought	May involve movement or one location Group relatively stable with some entering or leaving Suggestions emerge which begin to extend ongoing play New objects/resource brought to play but may not become integral to play Sporadic evidence of shared understandings of goal orientation Role play may be evident with some combined dramatic intent Interruptions/altercations may be evident when play returns to social Adult intervention seldom sought	Players remain predominantly in one location Shared understanding of goal orientation Players remain until goals achieved; new goals identified A highly imaginative use of ideas and materials as play themes are taken on board and explored Players seek additional resources to extend their play themes Role play has clear dramatic aspects A relative absence of play noises Absorption in task with extended levels of concentration Altercations are resolved in play as problem-solving activity Play achieves a finish product (where design is involved) Adult intervention not sought until completion

Comments and records (e.g. information about individual children, ideas for developing Area of Provision in focus and associated resources, location, extensions, adult intervention, class/group discussions):

Identify play domain (including 'moving towards'):	Associative	Social	Highly Social	Cooperative

3   reflecting on the short-term planning implications for curricular provision, i.e. planning with the Foundation Stage Curriculum in mind and combining this with children's interests and preoccupations to reinforce their learning opportunities.

In these respects, the Social Play Continuum serves a triple function – more of this a little later.

Drawing on the many observations that have been undertaken in developing the Continuum, Side 2 describes the characteristics of the play in each of the domains so as to complement the earlier focus on language and activity. It aims to elaborate on the necessarily brief language/action descriptors of Side 1. It aims to help the observer to be reflective (and it's at this point that paired discussions can be so beneficial), to recall events and responses from children with whom they are familiar – but about whom they may well be surprised.

In making a judgement about the dominant domain, a little pragmatism could be called for. For example, sometimes it is impossible to watch all the playing children; two or three groups of interactors might be engaged in one Area of Provision. The observer may select a particular grouping but then change to another grouping because it looks more interesting or because a child comes along about whom they wish to know more, for example for profiling purposes. Selecting a domain is a 'best fit' activity where observers seek to be as precise as possible and which can, as the sheet indicates, incorporate a 'moving towards' judgement, either 'up towards' or 'down towards'.

Some of these characteristics have been drawn out in the detailed scenarios of Chapter 1. Side 2 of the Continuum also aims to draw attention to the impact of altercations on the developing play. This should help observers to recall and recognize this aspect as influential on the emerging levels of reciprocity and momentum-building. It will also support reflection on the kinds of events that create altercations and whether these might be obviated in a development of the Area of Provision (for example giving the children more space, speaking to the class about 'cooperation'). Side 2 also draws attention to adult interventions in the Social, Highly Social and Cooperative Domains. Children tend to draw an adult's attention to the play when the altercation disrupts the play. Altercation disrupts momentum and we can see that play may return to a previous domain. In the Cooperative domain, children tend to resolve their own altercations so as not to interrupt the momentum; this becomes a form of problem solving, requiring negotiation and compromise – sophisticated communicatory skills and integral to cooperative activity. Players tend to call on an adult only when, for example in construction play, their design is complete and they want to be praised and receive some recognition for their achievements.

At the bottom of Side 2 is a small space to allow observers to record some of the reflections and decisions that might emerge in this post-observation period. Some aspects of this have been illustrated in Chapter 1 and further discussion is provided in Chapters 3 and 4. It is perhaps worth mentioning at this point that it is often useful to have additional sheets of plain paper handy alongside the Continuum to record the detail of some aspects of observation; for example, interesting exchanges of dialogue or the incorporation of new resources at particular points in the play.

In concluding Chapter 2, I want to offer an overview of observational activity while using the Social Play Continuum. Table 2.3 has been developed from the post-observation reflections and from the discussion at project meetings that accompanied

Table 2.3 The benefits and challenges of observing children's play and of shared reflection

Benefits	Challenges
Children quite quickly come to understand that they should leave the observers alone.	The effects on children of being observed may depend on how the adult describes their forthcoming behaviour to them. Sometimes the children have to be reminded not to approach the adults.
The children may be aware of being observed but it does not seem to affect their play.	It's sometimes difficult, as an adult with responsibility, not to be distracted by unrelated activity.
You learn that, left alone, children often solve their own altercations.	You sometimes want to intervene in the ongoing play or with play elsewhere.
Watching for long periods gives much useful information about the nature of play.	Watching for long periods may not be possible when alone in the classroom.
Specific information is gained about individual children and this can be surprising.	You need a sufficiently long period of observation to learn how momentum grows and is sustained. This also gives confidence in moving to higher domains on the Continuum when recording. This may not be achieved with a brief 'snapshot' of observation.
Specific information is gained about how Areas of Provision and resources can be used by imaginative/creative individuals who may be natural leaders of play. (The term *resources* describes supplementary materials such as fabrics, play people/cars in the sand, funnels in the water.)	Watching for long periods requires considerable concentration; sometimes it gets a bit boring.
The research has encouraged a focus on the range of types of provision being made available on a regular basis.	The play can break into smaller groups and it is difficult deciding which one to watch.
Insights are gained into how different Areas of Provision and different resources are productive in helping children extend and develop their play.	Hearing the dialogue is crucial but sometimes difficult.
Ideas emerge about the location of Areas of Provision.	Sometimes the room layout seems to inhibit fruitful developments in the play and then I feel a bit guilty for not seeing this before.
The post-observation discussions are helpful in a number of ways relating to the development of Areas of Provision, the needs and interests of individuals and supporting children in becoming cooperative.	Solitary observations could not accommodate post-observation discussions.

continued on next page

Ideas emerge about extending the provision of resources.	Budgets may not be available to support the extension of materials for Areas of Provision or for resources.
The Continuum becomes easier to use with regular use.	At first, the Continuum seems complex to use.
Using numbers rather than ticks helps to recognize the ebb and flow of play – we began to record the individual categories in sequence, numerically.	You sometimes forget which number you're on and use it twice.

the research. This overview precedes a more detailed focus, in the next chapter, on the practicalities of using the Continuum in early years settings.

A note about the research

Chapter 1 gave some detail on funded research that was undertaken in five reception classrooms. To reiterate briefly, the small but sufficient funding allowed the teachers to buy in half a day of classroom cover to allow for paired observations of each of the five Areas of Provision. We would observe in pairs, using the Continuum and recording children's conversations on plain paper. We would categorize the play, independently of each other, using the four domains of the Continuum. We would then come together to share our categorizations and discuss observations. In terms of testing the validity of the schedule, this joint research was reassuring.

Out of 63 paired observations and categorizations, only in five cases did we differ on the domain in which we initially located the play. To some extent, this differing selection of domain was not especially important except that we were testing the validity of the Continuum as a potential tool for others to use. What proved to be interesting were the discussions that subsequently took place to justify our personal decision-making. As we compared our choices of action and language on the Continuum, we engaged in in-depth and detailed discussions about the nature of the play we had observed. The discussions helped us to become more familiar with the Continuum as we each re-engaged with the observed play. It provided prompts for recognizing the skills and interests of individual children. Also, as was evident in Chapter 1, from these reflections, ideas about the development of Areas of Provision emerged.

One especially interesting aspect of this type of observation was that as an 'outsider' I did not know the children and so could be especially objective in my observations. The teachers recognized that they brought particular kinds of preconceptions about individual children to their observations and, as has already been noted, could be surprised by individual action and interaction. But in addition, the teachers also brought important knowledge of the child's context that I, as outsider, could not know. This proved to be an important dimension of the observation and of the post-observation reflections that will be illustrated in forthcoming examples.

The benefits and challenges of observing play as presented in summary form in Table 2.3 will be discussed in further detail in the next chapter.

Chapter 3 looks at these aspects in more detail. It explores the potential for creating opportunities in early years settings for staff to make extended, rather than brief, observations. I am often asked how long and how often I think observations of play should be. I recognize that contextual circumstances vary but as a general rule, I think half an hour per observation, at least twice a week is a good aim, but may not always be attainable. It also suggests ways in which practitioners might work together to make and then jointly reflect on their paired observations. Areas of Provision continue to be illustrated.

Chapter 3 also introduces a new Area of Provision. It tells of the events that led up to the emergence, during the research in reception classrooms, of the 'whatever you want it to be place' and gives some examples of it 'in action'.

Using the Social Play Continuum

Chapter 3 begins by looking at the development and purposes of practitioner research, recognizing classroom observation, whatever its purposes, as essentially a research-based activity. The chapter goes on to focus a little more on pupil assessment, and potential links with and some reservations about the Foundation Stage Profiling. It continues to explore pupil observations as an important source of information and, as promised at the end of the previous chapter, takes the benefits and challenges and explores them in greater detail so as to be supportive of practitioners in this complex activity.

Practitioners as researchers – insights into learning and teaching

Practitioner research is now a well-established and widely recognized pathway to professional development, although this has not always been the case. Its roots in this country can be traced back to the Action Research movement of Lawrence Stenhouse at the University of East Anglia in the late 1960s and work in secondary schools (Stenhouse, 1975). Later advocates developed approaches to Action Research (Elliott, 1980, 1985; Kemmis, 1981; Whitehead 1985, 1987; Carr and Kemmis, 1986; Simons, 1987; Lomax, 1989; Oja and Smulyan, 1989). A wide range of publications have brought about a better understanding of how personal research, in classrooms and other educational settings, can improve professional practice and also contribute to existing bodies of knowledge.

Practitioner research is a personal activity and is rooted in the control and ownership of participating individuals to design and direct the research at their own volition and, if they wish, in confidence; there should be no automatic assumption of discourse or dissemination. Action Research offers a cyclical approach to the investigation of personal practice leading towards practice enhancement, something similar to the Plan–Do–Review cycle that many early years practitioners know from the High/Scope curriculum. This repeated engagement allows the practitioner to delve a little deeper each time around, and, as confidence grows and expertise deepens, reflection-on-action becomes more meaningful in personal development terms, leading to changes and improvements in practice as the action researcher becomes willing to take some necessary risks by introducing new approaches and strategies into her/his repertoire. Risk-taking has always been an integral part of practice enhancement for teachers and others who work with children (Broadhead, 1995b).

Becoming and being collaborative

The passage of time has shown that collaborative research and evaluation activity can be more satisfying and productive for practitioner researchers. Collaboration can help sustain momentum by building in opportunities for 'reporting back' on how the work is going, and it can also better facilitate reflection than can solitary enterprise (Holly and Southworth, 1989). Reflection takes 'reporting back' a little further. Discussion becomes like that undertaken between myself and the teachers as we evaluated the Continuum, discussed the children's activities, needs, strengths and interests and thought about ways of improving the Area of Provision in focus. Reporting back has a strong descriptive dimension, whereas reflection incorporates an analytical dimension as the discussion interprets behaviours and seeks related meanings that have real implications for further action and/or understandings.

An important part of successful working partnerships between 'insider' practitioners and 'outsider' researchers working in this way is the extent to which the 'outsider' understands the culture and activity where observations and reflections are ongoing. 'Outsiders' can have such understanding arising perhaps from previous working experiences of these contexts or from considerable familiarity with the contexts being researched. Practitioners researching together are very likely to have shared understandings, and articulating these understandings can deepen them and inform practice, but such partnerships are by no means straightforward (Broadhead, 1989).

Practitioner researchers collaborating with colleagues or with 'outsiders' with a view to evaluation, reflection and development of practice has become an established format for higher degree work (Nias and Groundwater-Smith, 1988). Here, 'outside' tutors support an individual focus on research activity with course design supporting dissemination and opportunities for shared reflections on data collection and practice implications. Also, there are now many publications which draw together practitioner research for wider dissemination. Early years and primary publications include Broadhead (1995a) and Webb (1990).

Persistence and advocacy have moved practitioner research into the mainstream despite past accusations that, as a research approach, it has lacked rigour, or that research activities by individuals or small groups of practitioners were unable to contribute to a wider knowledge base concerned with understanding the complexities of teaching and learning.

Building on this move into the mainstream and recognizing the impact of practitioner research on personal, professional development, the Teacher Training Agency (TTA) was given a remit for encouraging practitioner research through its Best Practice Research Scholarships (BPRS) and the Networked Learning Community initiative. The former initiative supports individuals and/or small groups of teachers in research-based activity and the latter brings a larger number of schools together in collaborative research enterprise aimed at improving teaching and learning by fostering school-based and school-networked research and dissemination communities. The BPRS ran for three years with the final cohort to conclude the initiative in December 2004. At the time of writing, the Networked Learning Community initiative is recruiting its second cohort.

Some concerns have been expressed at government interest in practitioner research as a tool for promoting practice enhancement. As stated previously, all kinds of practitioner research were originally conceived of as empowering practitioners, of giving them the means of taking control of their own professional development and, if practitioners wished, of contributing through publications and dissemination to the discourses of theory-building.

As outlined in the introduction, my own interests in how children become sociable and cooperative grew out of practitioner research undertaken for a Bachelor of Arts degree and then further developed at Master's level. I would locate both pieces of work within the practitioner research paradigm (rather than the action research paradigm) because I was studying children's play rather than actively seeking to improve my own practice through action research. I have no doubt that the research did improve my practice when I subsequently returned to full-time teaching, but this was not its primary purpose at the time. Similarly, when the funding was secured to work with reception teachers and then Year 1 teachers, their participation was primarily as co-researchers in testing the validity and usefulness of the Social Play Continuum. However, the reception teachers' comments during interviews conducted after our joint research had been completed, revealed some of the ways in which their engagement as practitioner researchers had enabled them to improve aspects of their own practice because the research had prompted them to rethink their understanding of the value of play and their role in promoting it. These reflections about impact on thinking and acting are shared later in this chapter.

The Social Play Continuum as a tool for research and pupil assessment

The Social Play Continuum can be used in any early years setting where Areas of Provision are available or are newly established for teaching and learning, because:

- it would support *practitioner research* by contributing to a better understanding of how young children become sociable and cooperative and how educators might respond in promoting the growth of sociability and cooperation
- it would support *action research* for one or a group of practitioners wanting to enhance learning through an evaluation of Areas of Provision in their own settings
- it would support *individual assessments of children towards profile completion* when used in relation to Areas of Provision because, as the scenarios in Chapter 1 have shown, the Areas of Provision give opportunities for children to experience the breadth of the Areas of Learning of the Foundation Stage Curriculum as they develop the knowledge, understanding and skills inherent in the early learning goals *and* beyond them.

The Social Play Continuum might therefore be used by practitioners in any of the following contexts:

1 by an individual practitioner interested in developing her/his own practice, or perhaps as part of their research within the context of a further qualification at a range of levels (for example, at NVQ, certificate, diploma or Master's levels and beyond)

2   by an individual practitioner or interacting colleagues (e.g. a teacher and teaching assistant, or colleagues in a pre-school or childcare setting) developing an assessment profile for a child, possibly one with special educational needs

3   by an individual practitioner or interacting colleagues towards the completion of the Foundation Stage Profile for a child at the end of the reception year – the Continuum-based observations would be an integral part of the evidence base which informed the summative decisions required for the Profile to be completed

4   by students in training for an early years qualification in their development of observational skills and an enhanced understanding of the impact of Areas of Provision on social and cooperative development for young children and in relation to the implementation of the Foundation Stage Curriculum; this context would provide an excellent opportunity for creating a community of researchers who could come together to discuss and reflect together on their observations and insights

5   similarly, qualified practitioners, engaged in continuing professional development (through taught courses in further or higher education or through local authority initiatives) could also create a community of researchers sharing insights across similar or different early years settings

6   a group of co-workers in one setting, or two geographically close settings, could make collective use of it to create a community of researchers; the staff of a day nursery/family centre or playgroup or a school staff – early years/Key Stage 1 – might use the Continuum as a basis for collaborative activity in their pupil assessments and their quality enhancement activities.

Observing children

In anthropological research, it is essential to study communities in context in order to understand, describe and generalize (within reason) from the detail and nuance of the community members' action and interaction. Ethnography is the branch of anthropology that offers scientific descriptions of individual human societies. Children at play are such a society – one that has been little researched in recent times. Observation is a scientific tool if it is well-structured, well-planned and systematically undertaken; if the outcomes are rigorously documented and open to scrutiny, it is a recognized and accepted methodology with a now well-established pedigree (Woodhead and Faulkner, 2000).

The Curriculum Guidance for the Foundation Stage (QCA, 2000) makes some references to the links between observation and learning. The document identifies practitioner observation and appropriate responses to children as a principle for early years education (p. 11) and offers a later, quite brief exposition of this principle into practice (p. 16). While these sections are welcome, these brief references are insufficient for embedding the principle and practices of observation into the repertoires of busy practitioners who may, because of other imperatives, have had little systematic exposure to learning how to observe in their initial training and educational programmes. Perhaps in recognition of this, the Foundation Stage Profile, introduced some three years later (QCA, 2003), recognizes observation as offering crucial insights into children's progress, with an accompanying video that suggests practitioners wear a tiara to denote to children that observation is under way and the adult should not be approached at this time.

QCA provides an end of Foundation Stage Profile for completion in relation to an individual child prior to transition to Year 1 and Key Stage 1. The procedure implies significant reliance on observational evidence being gathered throughout the Foundation Stage, although the document itself talks only about the final year (QCA, 2003:3). This raises issues about assessments for younger children given that assessment-related activity offers a crucial link between planning and appropriate provision. In addition, the related recording processes which practitioners might use at any point in the Foundation Stage are not made clear. QCA leaves it to local authorities by stating: 'Schools may choose their own recording systems based on the Early Learning Goals' (QCA, 2003:3). Many local authorities are developing these to manifest the Stepping Stones as targets for achievement. Their completion, as with the Foundation Stage Profile, requires observationally based evidence gathering. It is in relation to this that the Social Play Continuum can assist practitioners in meeting these particular requirements, developing their provision and deepening their own knowledge and understanding of the relationships between play and learning.

There is a danger inherent in a target-based approach to assessing learning which links back to the climate in which early years provision has more recently developed in this country (considered in Chapter 1) and which may continue to prevail whenever settings find themselves accountable via an inspection process (however self-evaluative and 'light touch' it might become). The danger is that observation is used *only* to assess whether a child has achieved the Early Learning Goals (the *summative* use of observation in early years settings) rather than being used to identify the child's *current achievements and interests* and to plan for further or related learning experiences (the *formative* use of observation). This formative process is reflected to some extent within the Stepping Stones, but inevitably these are far too brief to reflect fully the extent and complexity of learning in each of the six Areas of Learning that make up the Foundation Stage Curriculum. This brevity in describing learning could undermine the use of observation as a means of helping practitioners to better understand how they can support learning, in that there are relatively few points of reference across the Stepping Stones to support practitioners in developing a full understanding of children's progression in each of these six Areas of Learning. For the Foundation Stage Curriculum to be helpful, this level of practitioner understanding would need to have been developed or to be developing elsewhere; it will not come from the assessment activity itself because there are inevitably too many gaps in the Stepping Stones to truly reflect the complexity of learning.

In making assessments of children's learning, Daniels (1993: 102) urges us away from the summative and towards the formative use: 'not towards yesterday but towards tomorrow in child development'. In this context, observation is only helpful to practitioners if they know what they are looking at, and if they can do so in a way that helps them better understand the complexity of what they are looking for, in terms of human development. Only then can observation be a truly useful tool to busy practitioners and only then can practitioners start to be surprised by what children do and by how they do it. Each time educators are surprised by what children can achieve, they are learning more about how children learn and about how they come to understand the world around them. The better we can understand the learning process, the more effectively we can support it. 'Ticking off' children's 'can dos' (making a summative assessment of the Early Learning Goals) tells us how effective the provision has been for children (hence its tendency to be associated with the accountability of inspection). This is perhaps a legitimate use of assessment but it requires a different and much narrower use of observation than that which is required when observation is used to help determine and sustain a learning environment which is responsive to children's needs and interests in supporting their formative development and progression in learning. Drury *et al.* (2000) and Dowling (2000), drawing on Katz's (1995) work, remind us that we cannot teach children everything they need to know. What we can do is nurture a disposition for learning and advocate that this become a major goal of education.

Before moving on to practicalities, let us look at some further extracts from the reception teachers who took part in the paired observations. Each of them was interviewed for a second time after the project had finished, to identify the impact, if any, of our joint research on their understanding and practice.

Reception teachers reflecting on observation

After talking about how play can assist children's fine motor skills and their technological and scientific understanding, I asked Jane from St Andrew's Primary School: 'Have you always been able to observe children's play in these Areas of Provision and see in that degree of detail what children have been doing?' She replied:

> Not until I've been doing this research. Before I was so wrapped up in 'spinning plates', making sure everybody was settled, that's the time when I might hear a few readers or get involved in an art and craft activity. Now I realize the value of observing children and hopefully I will continue to do observations. I've seen different aspects of children's development. I have one little boy whose academic achievement is slow going at the moment, but when I've seen him play, I've realized that this little boy is very highly skilled, his interactions with other children, the way that he motivates other children to be involved in the play, his speaking and listening skills and I may have made assumptions on his academic achievements and thought 'this boy is not making progress, he's had six months with me and he's not reading' but now I know his speaking and listening skills are at a much higher level than some children who are good readers. I'm seeing his development in a more balanced way. Without these observations, it's parents' day tomorrow and I would have been saying to his mother 'I'm concerned about his development' and I am still concerned about his reading but I can also be very positive about his many skills.

Similarly, in post-project discussions, Rose, at Heartland Primary School, identified what she had learned as a result of her detailed observations. Her response shows insights, surprises, and as with Jane above, Rose feels she can now share this broader perspective on children's learning with parents:

> I've learned how important it is to give their play time. I've also learned that children don't have to be talking to each other to be cooperating. I've learned a lot about the children in my class, it's been quite an eye opener and also how well they work with other children. We all know the dominant ones and the quiet

ones, but some of the others, it's been great to see how they have come on and I hadn't really realized it until I observed. It's really powerful with parents to be able to say, look, I've seen this happening. Our parents tend to want to see writing and such and now I can point to this research to talk about their child's developing cooperative skills.

In her reflections on personal impact, Catherine at Royal Whittington could also identify insights in relation to offering Areas of Provision in the classroom. This first comment illustrates how regular observations have given Catherine some generic insights – 'how play moves and changes' – while also helping develop her confidence in making large construction available in the classroom:

> Overall I'd say this has been very valuable and interesting to see how the play moves and changes. We really should try to build more regular observations into our timetable. One of the things I've really got over is my anxieties about using the blocks. I used to worry much more about accidents. I encourage supply teachers who come in to cover for us to be less anxious also. It's surprising how teachers do worry about block play until they really see how children use them.

In this later reflection, Catherine is looking to the future and how she might build on the observation experiences in her planning and classroom organization. Recognizing that she won't have an 'outsider' to work with, she is beginning to think about working with others:

> I think we need to develop the sand play next and it may be because I'm not as confident, we've decided to focus on it in our planning next term. I want to involve the teaching assistant in observations of the sand and water tray when we try them in their new positions.

Amy at Blue Grass Infant School talked frankly about some of her earlier reservations about such intensive involvement in classroom observations, and illustrates the confidence she now feels she has to, if necessary, 'defend' the presence of play in the classroom. In Chapter 1, Amy had talked of the 'tension' of trying to balance 'all the other things you are having to try and fit in'. Post-research, she reflected:

> I wouldn't ever take any of these activities away from my classroom now; I'd defend them to death. I was a bit apprehensive about the value of it all at the beginning and the requirements on me but I've thoroughly enjoyed it. I feel as though I've been given permission to focus on play even though I've always believed in it.

This final, brief comment from Angela is a reminder of how important it is to practitioners for their senior managers to understand and support practitioner research and observation; more especially, perhaps, when it is conducted within a climate that might prompt practitioners to perceive that there may be some controversy associated with what they are doing – although hopefully this feeling will diminish as the video associated with the Foundation Stage profiling and assessment becomes more widely viewed. Each of these reflections has illustrated how the participants now feel empowered to take risks, both in a prevailing climate and in their own practice. In this final comment in this section, Angela reminds us that such risk taking needs support and insight from heads and managers:

> It's been good to watch individuals undisturbed. I've been pleased that the heads have come to our project meetings to talk about the needs of young children also.

Getting started – observing children's play

> When adults seek to learn about and from children, the challenge is to take the closely familiar and render it strange.
>
> (Thorne, 1993: 12)

Chapter 2 concluded with a chart that came out of discussions at project meetings concerning the benefits and challenges of observing while also being responsible for the education and care of young children. We learned a few more things along the way that allowed the observations to progress without interruption. Some of our observational approaches were especially refined when the research moved into Year 1 classrooms because there was no additional cover at this point and it was essential to rely on aspects of classroom organization and on the preparation that was offered to the children about this unfamiliar role that familiar adults would be taking.

The next section looks at successful approaches to getting started and sustaining observations and incorporates, in each section, extracts from the 'Benefits and Challenges' table. It is followed by further examples of completed observation schedules along with a description and interpretation of the play.

Creating the time to watch, listen and learn

Familiarity and autonomy for children

Children quite quickly come to understand that they should leave the observer alone.	The effects on children of being observed may depend on how the adult describes their forthcoming behaviour to them. Sometimes the children have to be reminded not to approach the adults.
The children may be aware of being observed but it does not seem to affect their play.	It's sometimes difficult, as an adult with responsibility, not to be distracted by unrelated activity.
You learn that left alone, children often solve their own altercations.	You sometimes want to intervene in the ongoing play or with play elsewhere.

- In all three settings – nursery, reception and Year 1 classrooms – the teachers explained to the children beforehand that they would be 'watching the play'. They avoided saying 'watching *you* play' as this might increase children's self-consciousness. They also explained why – 'because it helps me to think about ways in which I can make the play better for you'. This explanation gave status both to the adults' work (they were not 'doing nothing') and to the play (it's important enough to watch).

- They also explained that they would need to 'write things down sometimes' and that if the children wanted to look at what was written and to talk about it, then they could do that later, after the watching was finished or at circle time (discussed further in Chapter 4). With younger children, some teachers found it helped the process if they wore a certain hat or a scarf (you quickly get over any self-consciousness – honestly!) and this acted as a reminder to children that for a short time, this adult was unavailable.

- In nursery/pre-school settings, there are often other adults available and children with particular needs can be directed to them. This is now increasingly the case in reception classrooms, with teaching support assistants working alongside teachers in increasing numbers. It is important to remember that the observations will not continue for long periods, but it is clearly also important that all adults are aware that one adult is 'out of commission' for a short period.

- If children forgot and did approach an observer, it helped to remind them of the current circumstances to either approach another adult or to manage for a short time longer rather than to try and respond quickly (unless an emergency of course); this reiterated the clear intention of the adult to 'watch' rather than to 'do' at this point in time.

- As time progressed in both the nursery settings and the reception classrooms, children were heard to say such things as 'you can't ask her, she's doing her watching' or 'you're not allowed to talk to her, she's got her hat on'. The children for whom it can be a little more difficult are the three-year-olds in nurseries or the young fours who want a conversation when they're ready for it. It may feel uncomfortable to put them off for a little while when language is *such* an important part of their development at this point, but conversations can be picked up at another point and watching is crucial too. But of course practitioners must decide as they feel comfortable.

- Similarly, in the early stages of observation, the teachers found themselves distracted by other activity in the room, or inclined to actually intervene in the play that they were supposed to be observing. They also discovered that, if they restrained their natural inclinations to 'go in and sort it out', the children were often able to sort it out for themselves. We went so far as to discuss in some cases (post-observation) whether some children might be creating altercations in order to test the adult's resolve and, in such cases, it certainly seemed wise not to be seen to respond immediately but rather to have a private word afterwards if this seemed feasible. However, once again, these also became issues for ongoing discussion at circle time (see Chapter 4).

- Once the children became familiar with this new role for adults, it became possible to get very close to their play without them seeming in the least self-conscious. One trick we learned was to remove eye contact whenever a child glanced over and to be 'busy' writing. If eye contact is prolonged, a child will take this to be an invitation to chat; when removed, s/he returns to the play. We also learned to pick our place carefully when sitting down to watch, to try not to be in a direct line from players, especially in the early days. We always sat on a chair and never stood (too obvious) or knelt (too uncomfortable). Comfort is important, as discomfort can be distracting and the temptation to finish early becomes too great.

- When we progressed to research in Year 1 classrooms, where there were no other adults, each of the teachers agreed to implement a different routine for the observation times. As part of the research project, they were setting up the Areas of Provision in their rooms to assess their suitability for this older age group. They consequently set up their classrooms with free flow, free choice activities for varying lengths of time. One teacher provided these every afternoon, another two teachers for two afternoons per week, and a fourth teacher for one afternoon per week in the first instance but gradually implemented it more frequently. The Year 1 teachers each found that free flow, free choice activities engaged the children to such an extent that they were seldom approached by children as they undertook their observations. If they were approached, a brief prompt/reminder was generally sufficient to send these more self-sufficient children back to their activities.

- It is perhaps worth bearing in mind Fisher's remarks (2002:116) and reiterating a point made previously. Drawing on Gura's work (1992) and Bennett *et al.* (1997), Fisher suggests that one reason why play does not hold its place in the early years classroom is that 'teachers do not have or make the time to gather the kind of observations that would give them the evidence they personally need to be convinced of the importance of play'. This reflection certainly chimes with some of the post-project comments included above.

Time to learn from observing play

The number of observations to be undertaken will depend on personal circumstances and willingness to persist. As remarked at the end of the previous chapter, a good length of time is half an hour and a reasonable frequency is twice a week. This might be more easily achieved if the observations are planned into the weekly outline by all involved adults. It was often the case in the Year 1 classrooms that half an hour was aimed for in the first instance but the observations were so interesting or the children so independent (or both) that they often continued for longer periods.

Watching for long periods gives much useful information about the nature of play.	Watching for long periods (half an hour) may not be possible when alone in the classroom.
Specific information is gained about individual children and this can be surprising.	You need a sufficiently long period of observation to learn how momentum grows and is sustained. This also gives confidence in moving to higher domains on the Continuum when recording. This may not be achieved with a brief 'snapshot' of observation.

Specific information is gained about how Areas of Provision and resources can be used by imaginative/creative individuals who may be natural leaders of play.	Watching for long periods requires considerable concentration; sometimes it gets a bit boring.

- The scenarios in Chapter 1 have illustrated how momentum grows as reciprocity increases and, then, how children progress to the more complex domains of Highly Social and Cooperative play. Think back to Chapter 1 and the play with the Lego® that transferred to the Brio® train track (Scenario 2 at Blue Grass Infant School). This play moved domains in a 'second' after 20 minutes of observation in the Social domain. Had our observations ceased a minute sooner, this would have been Social play rather than Highly Social. We were also conscious of how it would probably have progressed to Cooperative had the bell not rung for 'play-time'.

- Sometimes of course, the play will cease before a half hour period has elapsed. In Scenario 1 (the home corner at Heartland Primary School), after 15 minutes, only one child remained in the home corner area. The decision then is whether to remain there and wait to see if others arrive or to move to somewhere where the play looks interesting. In this case, Rose and I elected to move because we had two Areas of Provision in focus for our observations that day, and the large construction was looking interesting. This means beginning observations while play is ongoing, but that's fine as long as we remembered to be patient in the identification of already established themes.

- So, be flexible but be disciplined. If the play seems a little repetitive, think about whether it's the resources that are limiting it or perhaps the location. The noting of the observation start and finish times, along with the noting of the Area of Provision, will allow comparable observation times across Areas of Provision to be monitored if it is important to do this within personal research.

- In terms of the relationship with Profiling and associated discussions with other adults, an occasional focus on LEA recording sheets, after observations with the Continuum are completed, should allow some information about individual children to be recorded. This information will accumulate over time.

- Earlier in the chapter, Amy talked about 'defending these activities to the death'. Catherine talked of becoming more confident in providing block play, and encouraging supply staff to continue this. Catherine also spoke of the perceived need to 'focus on the sand play next' and of 'involving the teaching assistant' in the ongoing observations. Jane and Rose spoke of new kinds of insights about individuals to share with parents.

- Just as language is crucial to a child's developing understanding, it is also crucial for the adult. Post-observation discussions allow practitioners to articulate and then internalize their new insights. These can then be re-articulated in other contexts where the educator seeks to be influential.

Improving Areas of Provision through observations and reflections

The research has encouraged a focus on the range of types of provision being made available on a regular basis.	The play can break into smaller groups and it is difficult deciding which one to watch.
Insights are gained into how different areas of provision and different resources are productive in helping children extend and develop their play.	Hearing the dialogue is crucial but sometimes difficult.
Ideas emerge about the location of areas of provision.	Sometimes the room layout seems to inhibit fruitful developments in the play and then I feel a bit guilty for not seeing this before.
Ideas emerge about extending the provision of resources.	Budgets may not be available to support the extension of materials for Areas of Provision or for resources.

The post-observation discussions are helpful in a number of ways relating to the development of Areas of Provision, the needs of individuals and supporting children in becoming cooperative.	Solitary observations could not accommodate post-observation discussions.

- In recognizing and being able to articulate the contribution of these Areas of Provision to children's learning and understanding, educators become able to influence the allocation of budgetary resources in school (to expand their Areas of Provision), able to describe and justify the changes to provision emerging from their observations (to support their bids to senior managers and compete successfully against subject-related allocations), and able to describe, justify and educate others who may not themselves have such extensive knowledge about the value of play in the development of learning and understanding in young children.
- We have long said in the early years that we are our own worst enemies in terms of being unable to defend the value of play; informed observations are the key to this defence and, more importantly, to the education of those whose perspectives on the importance of play would benefit from expansion.
- When we first began the observations in the reception classroom, we used the methods I had used when observing in nursery classrooms; a tick was placed against the action or language as observed. While working with the reception teachers, it occurred to me that this method gave no detail about the flow of the play. Consequently I began using numbers (illustrated below) and some of the reception and Year 1 teachers used this method also.
- The numbers could then also correspond with recording of the dialogue/conversations on the plain pieces of paper that came to accompany the schedule as supplementary data collection. This was far more helpful in the post-observation reflections, both in our paired discussions and later when I was reflecting alone on

The Social Play Continuum in use

The Continuum becomes easier to use with regular use.	At first, the Continuum seems complex to use.
Using numbers rather than ticks helps one to recognize the ebb and flow of play.	You sometimes forget which number you're on and use it twice.

the data because it gave more accurate detail on these events rather than relying too substantially on imperfect memory.

- One of the Year 1 teachers developed possible recording techniques even further when she identified the strategy of placing a child's initials against the numbers on the Continuum. This allowed her to track individuals. As well as supporting Foundation Stage Profiling, this approach is especially useful if the Continuum is being used to assess children in relation to particular concerns about aspects of their development.

The next section takes a first look at a completed schedule and accompanying notes. The following scenario was observed in the reception class at Royal Whittington Primary School with Catherine. As well as illustrating the recording process and the flow of and interpretations of the play, this scenario is also interesting because:

- Catherine and I were watching for 20 minutes before we realized what the play theme was (genies and monsters)
- the post-observation reflections gave some serious food for thought on issues relating to noise levels in children's play and on the dangers of (wrongly) interpreting play from a distance without the benefit of the insights that extended and detailed observation can offer in understanding play and learning.

After the observations, Catherine and I agreed that this play had been Highly Social although we also felt that had there been more time for the play to continue, it may have progressed to Cooperative. We were also very aware that our late understanding of the genie theme (number 37 on the Continuum – play was nearly at an end) might have prejudiced this decision, but when we took account of the characteristics on Side 2 of the Continuum we felt that, overall, we were happy with this designation although there's a definite 'Moving Towards' inherent in our decision. Some of our reasoning is explained in the post-observation reflections.

First of all, the completed Continuum (Side 1) is presented. This is followed by a more detailed description of the play, similar to the format used in Chapter 1 (using description and interpretation). This time, however, the description of the play is directly linked to the numbers used on the observational schedule to give some sense of the flow of the play.

The play was already ongoing when Catherine and I sat down to watch it. As is noted (GGGB), three girls and a boy were playing with the dry sand. They had a range of resources in the sand, including a sand wheel, some funnels, spoons, small spades, shells and pebbles.

The Social Play Continuum – Side 1: a tool for play observation, pupil assessment and evaluation of Areas of Provision

Observation start time: **1.45pm**	Children entering play: **GGGB** (when obs. start) **B B**
Area of provision: **Dry sand**	Children leaving play: **B B**
Observation finish time: **2.10pm (tidy-up time)**	

L = Language   A = Action observed   L/A = Language and Action combined

RL = Reciprocal language   RA = Reciprocal Action   RL/RA = Reciprocal language and reciprocal action combined

ASSOCIATIVE DOMAIN

A: Looks towards peers

A: Watches play

A: Imitates play

A: Object offered, not accepted

A/L: Object taken, altercation

A: Parallel play period

L: Self-talk

A/L: Comment on action directed at peer; peer does not respond **6**

SOCIAL DOMAIN

A: Smiling

A: Laughter **32, 34**

L: Play noises, play voice **2**

RA: Eye contact made **11**

A: Object taken, no altercation

RA: Object offered and received

L/A: Consent sought and object accessed

L: Approval sought, not given

RL: Approval sought and given **17**

L: Instruction given, no response **7**

L/RA: Instruction given, positive response **1, 4, 8, 18**

L: Question asked, no response

RL: Question asked, response given

L/RA: Comment on own action/ described intent directed at peer, peer looks **3, 5, 9**

RL: Comment on own action/ described intent directed at peer, verbal response

HIGHLY SOCIAL DOMAIN

RA: Offering/accepting of objects evident

RL: Dialogue a mix of activity related and non-related but a theme is evident

RL: Comment on own action/ described intent with acknowledgement leading to extended exchange **15, 25**

RL: Sporadic dialogue develops role play themes **13, 19, 26**

RA/L: Eye contact/laughter (play noise) combined as behavioural cluster **27, 30**

RA/RL: Brief reciprocal sequences, e.g. giving/following instructions, seeking/giving approval, offering/accepting objects, asking/answering questions **16, 21, 22, 23, 29, 35**

RL/RA: New ideas or resources have impact on developing theme

COOPERATIVE DOMAIN

RA: Offering/accepting objects sustains/extends play theme

RL: Sustained dialogue is activity related and clear theme(s) emerge **20**

RL: Explanations/descriptions utilized **12, 14, 35, 36**

RL/RA: New idea/resource extends play and is sustained

RL/RA: Children display a shared understanding of goals **10, 24**

RL: Offering and accepting verbal help

RA: Offering and accepting physical help **31**

RL/RA: Verbal and physical help combined

RL/RA: Problem identified and solved

RL/RA: Sustained dramatic scenarios enacted linked to play theme(s) **37**

Emergent play themes noted:

Turning wheel. Monsters. Genie to save them from the monster.

Careful readers will note that there is no number 33 on this sheet – my omission during observations.

In the early part of the observations, the children are interacting but this is relatively infrequent. Each of the four seems preoccupied with their individual activity although there is some evidence of some degree of reciprocity with positive responses to instructions given and children looking across as someone comments on action.

Numbers 1–9 are all in the Social domain of single actions with limited reciprocity. One comment on action, although directed at a peer (6) elicits no response.

Two of the girls begin turning the sand wheel very quickly by putting sand through the top of the sand wheel. They have made this difficult by piling several pebbles and shells in the opening to the sand wheel. The third girl instructs them: 'You keep it going and I'll get more things', and turns to select pebbles and shells from the tray. The two girls keep dropping the sand through the restricted opening of the wheel. The boy gives instructions to the girl about which pebbles and shells to select. They seem urgent and focused: 'Keep it going, don't let it stop', referring to the turning wheel. The play is quite noisy, with all four voices raised at some point.

Number 10 is noted as the four seem to have a shared understanding of what needs doing. From this point until *number 20*, the recording shows a movement across the Highly Social and Cooperative domains as the play is observed and decisions made. This period lasts several minutes.

A fifth player, a boy, enters the play. After a few seconds, play stops and one girl says: 'You have to go out, only four allowed, only four'. There is some discussion of and pointing to the notice which states: '4 in the sand'. Further discussion and she says again: 'One person has to go, you can only have four' and orders the new boy out.

This is at *number 21* on the sheet. *22 and 23* are entered while a parallel discussion begins about whether or not he can stay in the sand. The four original players sustain their interactions about the turning wheel as well as intermittently stopping their play to discuss his presence.

continued on next page

He goes and they briefly discuss: 'we're right, we're not lying'. He returns at about 22 and says: 'I'm five, I don't have to leave', apparently mistaking the numbers who can play for age. The playing boy says: 'And I'm four' and a girl says: 'And I'm two' and laughs. The unwanted boy watches for a while and the others stand around and partly resume their play. He leaves and play returns to the previous vigour.

One girl draws a heart on the floor of the sand tray and calls to the others to look (number 25). This leads to a shout: 'The monster's here' (number 26) with lively discussion on this theme. One girl crawls under the sand tray and begins banging on the bottom of it. The two above remain anxious to ensure the sand keeps flowing: 'put a finger in'; 'hurry, it's running out'. The boy is putting sand in the wheel with some urgency.

The play moves quickly to the Cooperative domain, with number 24 being entered after a minute or so as the four children quickly return to their previous play.

Number 27 in Highly Social shows eye contact, laughter and play noises as a combined cluster.

The girl bangs again on the underside of the tray, laughing and calling something inaudible.

This is noted in Social as numbers 32 and 34.

She then explains to others, almost in narrative style, that the monster is coming (we now realize that this is the banging on the bottom of the sand tray). It also becomes apparent that the sand through the wheel is designed to 'invoke' the genie to come and save them.

Numbers 35 and 36 reflect this new observer understanding of the play, and number 37 shows a re-interpretation of the purpose of the previously observed play. Just as we realized this, the supply teacher announced that it was tidy-up time.

Post-observation reflections

- Some attempts at recognizing the play theme(s) are made but, as noted above, it is not until point 37 that we fully grasp the holistic and integrated aspects of the play. The whole scenario is concerned with the monster–genie theme but because the children have not needed to communicate directly on this matter for over 20 minutes, we, the observers, had been unaware. A 'shared understanding of goals' had been noted at 10, when we had observed the wheel being turned, but we were still without a unifying play theme at this point.

- This prompted us to reconsider our points 1–9. Were these in fact part of a 'reciprocal sequence' and worthy of categorization in the Highly Social domain? Possibly, and this once again reiterated the importance of seeking to recognize the ongoing play theme even if, on first watching, there does not seem to be one in evidence.

- Similarly, with the following points:

  16: Highly Social
  17: Social
  18: Social
  19: Highly Social

  Post-observation reflection prompted us to acknowledge that we might have undervalued the complexity of this play as we had for points 1–9. This does not invalidate in any way the decisions made while observing, but rather illustrates the place of discussion in re-evaluating those decisions once adult knowledge increases and perceptions alter through further observations.

- The noise levels were quite high during this play due to the banging on the bottom of the sand tray and the excited voices. Catherine remarked that more than once she had been tempted to intervene to reduce noise levels but was determined to remain in 'observer' mode. She did say that had she not been in observer mode, she felt that she would most definitely have intervened: 'I would probably have looked across and perhaps come over and said something like "do you think you could keep the noise down a bit?"' She admitted that with her current understanding of the play, she felt that such a response, to quieten the play, would have been a mistake. She hoped that this observation experience would prompt her to 'watch and assess' when any future, similar interventions relating to noise levels might seem appropriate. We both recognized that it was yet again our limitation in not knowing the play theme that had contributed to what Catherine now saw as an inappropriate 'instinct' on her part.

- Once Catherine recognized the play theme, she was able to link it with literacy activities in the preceding days. The children had been listening to and writing about fairy stories. This perhaps explained their preoccupations with and absorption in genies and monsters. Here were recent experiences and shared understandings being re-enacted in the sand tray. This insight contributed to Catherine's (and my) better understanding of how Areas of Provision can allow children to re-engage with their curricular experiences at their leisure. Further examples of this are examined in Chapter 5.

- Catherine recognized that the invoking of the class rule 'four only in the sand' had interrupted the play, although ultimately it had not prevented the playing children from developing their play. We discussed whether the rule was needed. The rule might have protected the play or, alternatively, the new boy might have helped to develop the play. Catherine felt at this point that she wanted to retain the rule but her colleague, June, at Royal Whittington had decided to experiment with its removal, as had the teachers in the remaining four reception classrooms, to see what would happen and to consider whether children would regulate their own numbers. This is further discussed in Chapter 4.

• We separately deliberated long and hard about the categorization of this play, moving between the Highly Social and Cooperative domains. When we came together, we decided on Highly Social but were never really certain how far this had been influenced by our own late understanding of the play theme, agreed by the children before our observations began. On balance we felt that there was no evidence of 'a highly imaginative use of ideas and materials as play themes are taken on board and explored'. We felt that there was no evidence of players seeking additional resources and that the dramatic aspects seemed sporadic rather than having 'clear dramatic aspects'. We felt that the characteristics of Highly Social play were a better fit, but this was debated at some length.

After the research was completed, when I returned to Catherine to ask her to reflect on which aspects of the research had had greatest impact, she once again recalled this sand play:

> One of the things I have learned from the observations is that the noises you some-
> times think they're making or the messing around you think they're doing, they're
> not. They're playing games. That time in the sand with the genie. Had I not been
> watching, my first thought when they were banging on the bottom would have
> been that there's a problem over there and I would have gone over and said some-
> thing like 'why are you making that noise?'

The next section introduces the 'whatever you want it to be place'. The section opens by explaining how the idea emerged at the final project meeting for reception teachers and participating heads and how it was then developed (and named by one of the children in Rose's classroom at Heartland Primary School). A second example of the Continuum in use is then offered, linked to this new Area of Provision.

The emergence of the 'whatever you want it to be place'

At the third and final project meeting, I shared an overhead with the group on which the observations in each of the Areas of Provision (across all the participating reception classes) as linked to the four domains of the Continuum had been categorized (Table 3.1).

When planning the observations, the teachers and I had each allocated periods when we would observe and record in two Areas of Provision (first one and then the other). After each observation, we would individually select our overall domain categorization and then discuss both the categorization and the observation more generally. In all but five of our paired observations, our individual (and initially private) categorizations were compatible. In compiling the chart that was shared at the project meeting, I subsequently used my own categorizations of these five observations.

Table 3.1 Observations categorized in each domain of the Continuum

Area of Provision	Associative Play Domain	Social Play Domain	Highly Social Play Domain	Cooperative Play Domain	Total for Area of Provision
Large construction		5	4	3	12
Small construction/ small world	1	6	6	3	16
Role play		10	1	1	12
Water		6	4	2	12
Sand		5	1	5	11
Total (including rough percentage of whole)	1 (1.3%)	32 (50%)	16 (25%)	14 (23.7%)	63 (100%)

Our observational timetable in each class should, in theory, have led to 12 observations in total for each Area of Provision across the six reception classrooms. Table 3.1 shows 16 observations for small world and only 11 for sand, with 12 for each of the remaining Areas of Provision. For small world, this was because some observations were relatively brief (because children left the area) but there would be other opportunities to return to observations of this area during the time it was in focus. In relation to the sand, in one of the classrooms, when it should have been an area in focus, it had been removed to another classroom (the reception teacher had forgotten that we were focusing on it at this time), so that opportunity was lost.

These tabulated findings prompted some interesting discussion at the project meeting.

- Most of the observed play was in the Social domain but the Highly Social and Cooperative when combined were almost equal to the Social domain totals. This reassured us that these Areas of Provision had the potential to support play at these higher and more complex levels in reception classrooms.
- Sand play had recorded the greatest proportion of overall observations in the Co-operative domain (5/11, 45 per cent), with large construction coming next (3/12, 25 per cent). This led into discussions about what it was that might help 'move the play along' into these more complex domains, something that is revisited in greater detail in Chapter 4.
- The group was very surprised by the role play findings. It had been anticipated, prior to seeing the table, that this would rank highly for supporting children's play in the Highly Social and Cooperative domains. Instead, the collated findings across the six reception classrooms had shown that Social Play was substantially prevalent in the role play areas and that this was the lowest 'scorer' for proportions of play in the Cooperative domain (only 9 per cent as compared with sand's 45 per cent and large construction's 25 per cent).

The role play areas had varied across the classrooms, with two home corners, a shop, a café and a party being *in situ*. As the group studied the table, Jane, from St Andrew's

Primary School, commented on the extent to which the sand and the large construction offered open-ended play materials to children. She had noticed how they could determine for themselves which play themes to pursue as the play progressed and developed and also how play themes had changed at the suggestion of individual children. On the other hand, a themed area such as a home or a shop, although it might chime with the children's prior and daily experiences, was more closed in its potential for stimulating or accommodating alternative play themes. This aspect is well illustrated by Rogers (1998), who offers a vivid description of reception children 'side-lining' the pet shop in order to re-acquire the supposedly out of bounds home corner. She reflects on this 'subversive' play as a logical and rather sensible pursuit of personal interests by children. Such reflections opened up the group's discussion to a consideration of what might be available to children in a 'non-themed' role play area. Rogers (1998) reflects on the possibilities of an empty space, but our thoughts turned elsewhere.

Ideas such as pieces of fabric, empty boxes, a clothes horse, hats and cushions emerged. The group found themselves thinking back to their own childhoods and to their children's childhoods to recall the creation of dens and secret places. The outcome of discussions was an agreement to extend the project. Each teacher would establish in their classroom what we referred to at this point as 'an open-ended role play area'. They would each determine which resources would be provided and the period of time for which it would be available to children. We agreed to extend paired observations, one more per class. The heads agreed to find some cover from budgets to pay for teacher release for paired observation and reflection. This would be done in the following term. We agreed to use the second half rather than the first half of term as the teachers would be receiving new children into class in first term and wanted some time to help these children to settle before continuing with their research into this new Area of Provision.

A new Area of Provision

We used the Continuum and additional pieces of plain paper to record our observations of the 'open-ended role play area'. Each teacher set up the area in her own way and developed and adapted it over the extended research period. This new Area of Provision wouldn't necessarily be available every day; the frequency of availability varied from class to class. Each teacher kept a record of what was introduced to the area and of how the children responded.

The following offers a description of this open-ended role play area in two classes, along with reflections that followed on from paired observations. Apart from changing the names and a little bit of grammatical 'tidying', this is offered here in the format in which it was circulated to all the teachers after paired observations in this new Area of Provision had been completed. Consequently, it is in a slightly different format from any that has been used previously, in that it:

- blends an overview perspective of each observation with some further detail of action and interaction and of dialogue
- highlights the play themes that emerged in each of the observations while simultaneously depicting the flow of the play

- illustrates some new areas into which our post-observation reflections were drawn as a result of the children's responses to this Area of Provision and the associated resources.

Each of the scenarios is introduced with a brief description of the context for the play; the observation sheet is also included for reference although no further references are made to this in the subsequent discussion.

Of the six observations undertaken in this new Area of Provision, four were categorized in the Cooperative domain and two in the Highly Social domain, leading us to consider that open-ended role play might have greater potential for promoting cooperative play than the themed role play observed previously.

Before moving on to the two scenarios, it is perhaps worth describing how this Area of Provision was named. It happened at Heartland Primary School, in Rose's class. The children had had regular access to the area over several days. Rose quickly became a convert to the area's potential as she witnessed the regular episodes of Highly Social and Cooperative play that were stimulated. She found that the play was occasionally quite boisterous, but felt that she did not wish to intervene regularly with requests to 'play quietly'. As an alternative to what she felt would have been a rather negative intervention, she introduced the opportunity to discuss the play more generally at circle time, and found the children were speaking and listening well at such times. In these discussions, Rose kept referring to it as the 'open-ended role play area' with the children. One day she remarked: 'I'm tired of calling it that; what shall we call it?' Jenny replied: 'It's the whatever you want it to be place, because it can be whatever you want'.

The 'whatever you want it to be place' in St Andrew's Primary School

This Area of Provision was established on the carpet in the classroom. The children had access to a wooden clothes horse, several pieces of fabric, pegs, cushions, plastic seats and buckets. They incorporated an empty, nearby table into their play – it starts out as a 'party'. When stacked, the related resources took up very little room on the carpet and did not prevent class discussions from taking place here at other times.

Both Jane and I independently categorized this observation as being in the Cooperative domain; the prevalence of the numbers on this observation sheet in the Cooperative domain illustrates the reasons for our decision.

The children had had access to the play for about two weeks when Jane and I undertook this paired observation.

- Number 1 on the Continuum can be found in the Cooperative domain and the observation finishes with number 37, also in the Cooperative domain.

The Social Play Continuum – Side I: a tool for play observation, pupil assessment and evaluation of Areas of Provision

Observation start time: **9.30am**   Children entering play: **GGGB**   Observation finish time: **10.25am**

Area of provision: **Open-ended role play**   Children leaving play: **NONE**

L = *Language*   A = *Action observed*   L/A = *Language and Action combined*
RL = *Reciprocal language*   RA = *Reciprocal Action*   RL/RA = *Reciprocal language and reciprocal action combined*

ASSOCIATIVE DOMAIN

A: Looks towards peers
A: Watches play
A: Imitates play
A: Object offered, not accepted
A/L: Object taken, altercation
A: Parallel play period
L: Self-talk
A/L: Comment on action directed at peer; peer does not respond

SOCIAL DOMAIN

A: Smiling
A: Laughter **5**
L: Play noises, play voice **10**
RA: Eye contact made **2**
A: Object taken, no altercation
RA: Object offered and received
L/A: Consent sought and object accessed
L: Approval sought, not given
RL: Approval sought and given
L: Instruction given, no response
L/RA: Instruction given, positive response
L: Question asked, no response
RL: Question asked, response given **11, 18**
L/RA: Comment on own action/ described intent directed at peer, peer looks **16**
RL: Comment on own action/ described intent directed at peer, verbal response

HIGHLY SOCIAL DOMAIN

RA: Offering/accepting of objects evident
RL: Dialogue, a mix of activity related and non-related but a theme is evident
RL: Comment on own action/ described intent with acknowledgement leading to extended exchange **9**
RL: Sporadic dialogue develops role play themes
RA/L: Eye contact/laughter (play noise) combined as behavioural cluster **3, 25, 31**
RA/RL: Brief reciprocal sequences, e.g. giving/following instructions, seeking/giving approval, offering/accepting objects, asking/answering questions **32, 33**
RL/RA: New ideas or resources have impact on developing theme

COOPERATIVE DOMAIN

RA: Offering/accepting objects sustains/extends play theme **15, 22, 36**
RL: Sustained dialogue is activity related and clear theme(s) emerge **4, 13, 20, 23, 28, 35**
RL: Explanations/descriptions utilized
RL/RA: New idea/resource extends play and is sustained **29, 34**
RL/RA: Children display a shared understanding of goals **17, 19, 30**
RL: Offering and accepting verbal help **37**
RA: Offering and accepting physical help **5, 6** (with clothes-horse)
RL/RA: Verbal and physical help combined
RL/RA: Problem identified and solved **7, 8**
RL/RA: Sustained dramatic scenarios enacted linked to play theme(s) **12, 27**

Emerging themes – several themes were pursued by children as the play progressed.

Party – one girl wanted this theme and suggested it at the beginning of play: 'We're having a party'. Others seemed less inclined to follow that route: 'No we're not', a second girl replied almost immediately. The first girl pursued her party theme independently and set out plates on the nearby table. One child from the group of four 'came' to her party briefly and then returned to play with the other two. The party girl also rejoined the group after pursuing her theme independently. At this point, the other children are tussling with the problem of getting the clothes horse to stay erect and then with the problem of getting the large pieces of cloth to stay in place with pegs. The girl who 'went' to the party subsequently reintroduced the party theme when the cave theme emerged a little later in the play.

House – the three children tussling with the clothes horse and fabrics are building a house. As they finally get the design they want and the fabrics in place they get inside and one declares: 'I think our house is too small'. The boy remarks: 'Well let's make a *tent*'. He begins to redirect; the others initially resist but then comply. A few minutes later, the boy remarks: 'Let's make a *cave*'. The other children seem non-committal but one girl replies: 'I'll get a table', to which the boy replies: 'You don't have tables in a cave'. She remarks: 'We need one for the party', which suggests some ambivalence to the cave theme perhaps. This is the girl who attended the party, not the one who instigated the theme. However, the girl who instigated the party theme, perhaps seeing 'an opening', quickly remarks: 'I'm getting dinner ready' and returns to her plates and food. She is clearly still in pursuit of her 'party' theme and seems prepared to have it redirected if there's a chance it can be incorporated.

At some point, inaudible to me, the cave has become a *car*. The boy seemed to take the lead in introducing and sustaining the new themes although it's not possible to confirm that the car theme was his suggestion. The clothes horse has been turned over with two girls helping the boy, and he declares: 'Now we need seats'. When the seats are placed in the car, a conversation develops between the 'party girl' who has joined the play and the boy. She sits in the front seat. He asks her to go to the back; she declines. He remarks (encouragingly) that the big ones always sit at the back. She remarks: 'We're the same size because we're both five my little choochy', and pinches his cheeks. But she does move and he gains access to the front seat to 'drive', eventually. At some point, the car has become a

Roller coaster – and stays as this for the remainder of the play. All four play for 20 minutes imitating a roller coaster and keeping the structure upright with their hands. The boy puts cloth over them and says: 'We're in a tunnel'. This is repeated several times amid much laughter. There are joint endeavours to redesign led by the boy. The 'party girl' also moves away to work with boxes and then experiments with incorporating her new design into the structure. She sits down and calls to the boy: 'Get in Dad, woahey'. He sits and then gets out again and explains his reasons for redesigning – he is trying to get a large cushion into the roller coaster. The party girl pulls it, trying to help him; another girl joins in. The party girl calls: 'Go on Dad', encouraging him and laughing. Then the girls try to push it out but playfully, laughing in a teasing way. He smiles and pushes back gently, saying: 'We do need the cushion in'. The play becomes boisterous but still controlled, with all children lying on their backs with their feet in the air. This is brief and they return to the roller coaster theme, with the cushion now inside the roller coaster as required by the boy. He is putting pieces of fabric over them again.

Play begins to become boisterous again, more so than last time. They tumble together, laughing. The clothes horse falls about them and one girl calls out from beneath the pile. They all stand with a bit of a struggle and the girl looks a little anxious but soon smiles. They stand and look at one another, smiling, and the boy remarks: 'I'll make it comfier for you'. They return to the structure and, quite quickly, it becomes boisterous again. This is the greatest intensity and Jane is looking anxiously at me as I have a better view of what is happening. I really want to see what will happen and the children, although very boisterous, seem to be exercising self-control so I offer a reassuring look and she remains seated. One girl then falls, another gets a 'body knock' from another child on the head. Immediately they stand, looking red and concerned. This passes very quickly; they smile at one another and one girl says: 'Eee I'm hot, let's take our cardies off, enough roller coaster for one day I think'. A few seconds later, the boy remarks: 'Let's make a cave this time'. They begin to design in a quiet way.

Jane and I discussed the following in our post-observation reflections.

- The themes seemed to reflect individual children's preoccupations and were taken up to greater and lesser extents by other children. Only two of the four players seemed to suggest themes, although some *were* introduced inaudibly. The party girl introduced her theme and it was sustained to some extent, but only by one other player. The other themes seemed to come from the boy. He returned to the cave after the boisterous play. It had not 'taken off' earlier as other children did not seem particularly interested in committing themselves to it. On this second occasion, no-one appeared to demur. Perhaps he had intuitively selected a good time to reinstate the cave theme.

- The introduction of the themes seemed to represent a trawl of individual experience along with an individual estimation of the extent to which the theme was being taken up by other players. The party girl was prepared to play alone and another girl joined her briefly; she reintroduced the party theme slightly altered to 'dinner' in a later attempt to reinstall it into the play. No one responded in a way that suggested they wanted to take up the theme, but this didn't prevent her from engaging with this theme.

- Manipulating the fabric with the clothes horse presented an ongoing challenge as the children sought ways of attaching the fabric to the wooden frame. One girl and the boy were especially preoccupied with this and tackled the problem in different ways. The girl tried pegging and persisted for many minutes until she succeeded; it was difficult because the wood was just a little too thick for the pegs and they kept flying off. The boy was trying to throw the fabric over the frame (potentially a better idea as it was a sufficiently large piece) but he did not put a sufficient amount over and the fabric continually fell back to the floor. Yet still he tried, and as he did so may have been learning something about the properties of different pieces of fabric. He needed help – someone to pull from the opposite side – but had not yet thought to ask for it. When he came later in the play to cover children in the roller coaster, he quickly selected a relatively heavy piece of fabric – ideal for the job as it draped around the children and did not slide away. Was this evidence of a growing understanding of the properties of these resources because of his earlier, quite extensive experimenting?

- The 'gender divide' seemed evident and yet the actions and language uses from the two dominant players (the party girl and the boy) seemed a powerful combination which contributed to the sustaining of the play. The boy initiated the greater number of themes; he redirected themes when they seemed not to be taken up or extended them when they seemed to be losing momentum. His ideas continually sustained the reciprocity across the four. The girls were facilitative, joining in with his suggestions when the theme was of interest, following his instructions, occasionally making their own suggestions and encouraging him with verbal and non-verbal responses.
- Jane was pleased in that one of the observed players was normally a very quiet girl in class but here she was animated and excited in her play. Jane remarked that this was 'another side to her personality in class; Mum says she's lively at home'.
- Jane spoke of her concerns about the children's safety during this play while it was ongoing but was pleased, with hindsight, that she had not intervened because these children had demonstrated that they were able to keep themselves safe and to self-moderate the 'excitement levels' of their ongoing play. Interestingly, there had been very little interest from other children in the class in this ongoing play, despite its boisterousness. One or two had stopped to watch in passing, but only briefly. Jane remarked that when it was first introduced, the majority of children had:
    (a) wanted to play in the area
    (b) watched the play for quite long periods when not a player – looking very much like the audience in a theatre, often pulling up chairs.
    Regular availability had diminished the competition to 'get in there' as children came to understand that the area was a permanent fixture and their turn would come. Familiarity had also gradually diminished the interest of non-players, although passing interest was often shown, as with this play.
- One of the early features that struck Jane about this play was how much it looked like 'play at home', rather than 'play in class'. Similar post-observation comment was made by other teachers and linked with the discussions at the final project meeting about their own play as children and their own children's play at home. The party theme had prevailed for several days prior to this observation. The party girl had made food at home and brought it into the area. The children had asked for plates and Jane had sent them into the store cupboard to see what they could find. They had found golden card circles and incorporated these into the play. In previous observations (as on this occasion), Jane had noticed that children seldom left this play area once they had started to play. She had also decided that she would restrict play to four players at a time until she became more familiar with the direction that play was taking.
- Jane commented on ongoing discussions between herself and the teaching assistant. They had talked at length about whether to intervene when they had seen children having difficulties manipulating the fabrics over the frame of the clothes horse. One possible way forward, they felt, might be to role model play with the fabrics themselves, pretending to play and finding ways of manipulating the fabrics. Jane felt that this approach seemed preferable to merely telling children how to solve the problem; to be dramatic rather than directly instructive. The observations also

revealed to Jane that the pegs she had provided were inadequate for attaching fabric to the frame. She subsequently provided bulldog clips, which were far more effective.

- Overall, Jane believed that the play was highly beneficial for the children, extending them in ways that other activities and experiences do not do. At the time of our paired observation, she was experimenting with putting in a range of different kinds of fabric of different weights into this Area of Provision.
- The 'whatever you want it to be place' began to challenge some of our previous conceptions about the characteristics of Cooperative play. We had previously thought of it as being relatively devoid of laughter and play noises, these being the domain of Highly Social and Social play. Here, the laughter was a direct response to the interactions while in character as jokes and humorous moments emerged, and to the excitement of the roller coaster which tilted and then fell, taking the children with it. We felt that the laughter was an integral part of the sustaining of the dramatic scenarios. It was our ongoing observations of this play that prompted a new entry in the Cooperative domain, the final one: 'Sustained dramatic scenarios enacted linked to play themes'. It was also these aspects that emerged more clearly when the play was observed in Year 1 classrooms.

Let us move on to look at another example of the 'whatever you want it to be place' where emotional needs are also met and where play themes change over time as the play flows along.

The whatever you want it to be place in Blue Grass Infant School

Here the children had access to cardboard boxes of varying sizes, plastic crates, storage boxes and pieces of fabric. Amy had located the Area of Provision in a corridor adjoining her classroom. This was quite a wide corridor and the children were familiar with opportunities to play in this area, although it was usually their large construction play that was located here.

We decided that this play was in the Highly Social domain. Although some of the action did move into the Cooperative domain, the play seemed a little bit too fragmented; continuity seemed difficult for the children to attain. New ideas emerged but then were replaced rather than sustained.

The play also broke into paired play and parallel play on occasions. Amy had watched some children during their play in this Area of Provision during the previous week, and had categorized that as Cooperative play. Her overall view at this time was that the play tended to be in the Cooperative domain. She was also reflecting on the extent to which individual children seemed to have positive or otherwise impacts on the level that the play reached, and this aspect is examined in the post-observation discussions.

- Number 16 is missing on this observation sheet.
- Number 1 is in the Social domain and number 45 in the Cooperative domain.

The Social Play Continuum – Side 1: a tool for play observation, pupil assessment and evaluation of Areas of Provision

| Observation start time: **1.15pm** | Children entering play: **GGGB** | Observation finish time: **2.30pm** |
| Area of provision: **Open-ended role play** | Children leaving play: **NONE** | |

L = Language   A = Action observed   L/A = Language and Action combined
RL = Reciprocal language   RA = Reciprocal Action   RL/RA = Reciprocal language and reciprocal action combined

ASSOCIATIVE DOMAIN

A: Looks towards peers
A: Watches play
A: Imitates play
A: Object offered, not accepted
A/L: Object taken, altercation
A: Parallel play period
L: Self-talk
A/L: Comment on action directed at peer; peer does not respond

SOCIAL DOMAIN

A: Smiling
A: Laughter **12**
L: Play noises, play voice **23, 24**
RA: Eye contact made
A: Object taken, no altercation
RA: Object offered and received
L/A: Consent sought and object accessed
L: Approval sought, not given
RL: Approval sought and given
L: Instruction given, no response **19**
L/RA: Instruction given, positive response **20, 22**
L: Question asked, no response **3, 4**
RL: Question asked, response given **2**
L/RA: Comment on own action/ described intent directed at peer, peer looks **1, 21**
RL: Comment on own action/ described intent directed at peer, verbal response **7**

HIGHLY SOCIAL DOMAIN

RA: Offering/accepting of objects evident **5, 6**
RL: Dialogue, a mix of activity related and non-related but a theme is evident **42**
RL: Comment on own action/ described intent with acknowledgement leading to extended exchange **10, 44**
RL: Sporadic dialogue develops role play themes **31**
RA/L: Eye contact/laughter (play noise) combined as behavioural cluster **9, 18, 30, 37, 40, 43**
RA/RL: Brief reciprocal sequences, e.g. giving/following instructions, seeking/giving approval, offering/accepting objects, asking/answering questions **17, 27, 29, 32, 41**
RL/RA: New ideas or resources have impact on developing theme

COOPERATIVE DOMAIN

RA: Offering/accepting objects sustains/extends play theme **26**
RL: Sustained dialogue is activity related and clear theme(s) emerge **15, 25**
RL: Explanations/descriptions utilized **8, 13, 28**
RL/RA: New idea/resource extends play and is sustained **34, 38**
RL/RA: Children display a shared understanding of goals **11, 45**
RL: Offering and accepting verbal help
RA: Offering and accepting physical help **14, 33, 39**
RL/RA: Verbal and physical help combined
RL/RA: Problem identified and solved **35, 36**
RL/RA: Sustained dramatic scenarios enacted linked to play theme(s)

The main theme was a *space rocket*; Ashley determined the theme and 'imposed' it on his peers by constantly repeating his suggestion until another child joined him in the space rocket play. It doesn't seem likely that the second child would have taken it up had he not wished to do so – on the other hand, he might have thought that his only alternative was to leave the area and perhaps the desire to stay was stronger than the desire to make something else. Ashley was very insistent.

Other themes came and went – there were two attempts at *the seaside* from one boy but they were not taken up (interestingly, some fabric had sea shells on it). Other themes were *witches and wizards*, then *vampires*, inspired also perhaps by some black fabric with silver moons and stars on it. The witches and wizards and vampire themes were sustained and interchanged as all four players became involved by wrapping themselves in fabric and following one another around the area, striking dramatic poses and stating their character and what the character was about to do. Maria (see below) joined in the play physically but did not speak.

There was also a *dead chicken* theme, which was interesting in that it involved an elective mute (Maria) and a confident and articulate girl, Josie – the two boys were only peripherally involved in this theme, which continued for about 15 minutes. Maria has language but chooses not to use it at school. She remained with the play throughout but did not speak. She became the dead chicken at Josie's instigation, who began to pull Maria along wrapped in fabric. She dragged Maria over to the boys to talk about what she was doing. There was a little bit of related discussion, but the two boys were immersed in their space rocket play at this time.

At one point, Maria was dragged to a box and told to get in and go to sleep. Another time she was placed in a box and told that this was the cooker and she was being cooked for dinner. This almost raised a smile from Maria, and was the only occasion that Amy and I saw any sign of response (other than her continued compliance) from Maria. Another time Maria sat by the 'computer' (the box she had previously 'slept in') and did her work, as instructed by Josie. Maria complied with every direct instruction and at no time did she seem uncomfortable or resistant. She never looked at Amy or me, and we were sitting quite close to the play area.

- In the post-observation reflections, Amy and I discussed how untypical it had looked to see children playing in this way in a school setting. Sometimes the area looked messy and the children's play may have appeared unstructured to a casual observer. The resources impose very little of a predetermined structure on the children; the fluidity of their themes is evident, as is the fact that they revisit these themes at intervals. There were few natural boundaries in the area where the children were playing. As we were observing, another class walked by on their way to the hall for their PE lesson. The passing children were clearly fascinated by the play, stopping to watch and bumping into the back of one another. The teacher remarked: 'Goodness, what's going on here?' and looked rather quizzically at Amy and myself. Amy replied: 'We're doing some research on play'.
- The two boys seemed to spend a lot of time investigating the nature and possibilities of the resources once the space rocket theme had finished. Although slow starting, it did continue for quite a long period between the two boys, with the girls participating for some of the time. Ashley introduced the computer theme that was later taken up again by Maria at Josie's instigation.

- At one point, three children (not Maria) were trying to enclose themselves within a box, contorting their bodies and squeezing themselves in, one seeming to take the idea from another. They seemed to be testing and investigating shape and space and sustaining a running commentary as they did so. On the one hand, the behaviour was interactive, highly social and occasionally cooperative. On the other hand, as with the 'dead chicken' play, on the surface it looked like 'messing around'. It was only the unremitting observation that revealed pattern, logic and investigation at work. The children seemed intent on discovering just how flexible these resources were and what kinds of interactions were possible with each other and with the resources.

- The group had several other periods of physical intimacy, curling up together, stroking one another's faces, lying together and putting their faces close together and talking quietly. Maria participated in all aspects except the talking. Amy and I reflected that while play of this kind might be a familiar experience in a home-based context, it was not usual to witness such long periods or such frequency of play of this kind in a school context. Yet it was clearly enjoyable for the four children and was very similar to intimacy observed at Heartland Primary in Rose's classroom, where, at one point, eight children had lain in a row, like spoons, each cuddling the one to their right as part of their 'sleeping on the train' theme. One boy had distributed pegs to everyone as their 'dummies' and they had each sucked and cuddled in perfect harmony. The whatever you want it to be place seemed to encourage quite high levels of affectionate physical contact. This was also to be the case in the Year 1 classrooms.

- Amy continued with the Area of Provision and the observations after this extension to the project had finished. She became especially interested in how children's personalities influenced the play and were influenced by the play. She had been especially surprised at the extent to which Maria had been happily complicit in the play. Prior to the observations, Amy had considered Ashley to be quite a dominant child but she had not fully realized the positive influence of his persistence and good ideas on other children. Perhaps such open-ended play gives children much more chance to 'be themselves', whatever that might be, within the confines of the classroom. Amy felt that this play would become a part of her continuing provision. She remarked also that it had the merit of being almost free to provide, with many of the resources being freely attainable.

Chapter 1 concluded with three emerging principles to underpin thinking about Areas of Provision:

- allowing children to sustain and develop their play
- recognizing and nurturing play themes
- fostering friendships for young children.

The remainder of Chapter 3 will briefly return to these underpinning principles of play provision and develop them a little further.

Allowing children to sustain and develop their play

The idea for the 'whatever you want it to be place' had arisen directly from reflections by project members (myself, the heads and the reception teachers) on the tabulated findings of play across the four domains of the Continuum. In some ways, this has been one of the most exciting outcomes of the research so far, an emerging idea that combines insider and outsider insights along with a child's matter-of-fact suggestion that was itself so simple yet so insightful.

When Jenny 'named' this Area of Provision she offered a very powerful personal perspective on how children might see the links between play and free choice. I would go even further and argue that she was articulating the potential in this Area of Provision for children to co-construct their curricular opportunities alongside the decisions taken by adults, in relation to children's learning experiences, every day. The themes emerge from the children's interests and experiences as they recognize and harness the potential of the resources available to them. Adults, on the other hand, can often predetermine play content by having certain kinds of expectations and plans regarding how children should be using their play opportunities to achieve certain objectives predetermined by adults.

On the one hand we might legitimately argue that this is what practitioners are trained and paid to do. But we can see also how adults' plans might suppress children's initiatives. In the same way that the Stepping Stones can only ever be a partial expression of the complexity of learning, adults can only ever partially imagine all that children might do and achieve when they play.

Recognizing and nurturing play themes

From the scenarios studied so far, it can be seen that some play themes become quickly established and flourish, others are engaged with for relatively brief periods, and others seem to be in the mind of only one player and offer limited opportunities for social activity (this doesn't make them less valuable as activities). When individual children connect with play themes, it is more likely that the play will progress into the Cooperative domain. In this domain, the children are using complex ideas and complex language modes on a regular basis. Not all participating players will necessarily be operating at the same levels of complexity, but while the modes are sustained, all are exposed to these levels, ideas and modes of interaction.

The themes are coming from a wide range of sources, some of which we can perhaps only guess at. Children are drawing on their curricular experiences from the more formally planned teaching–learning opportunities. They are drawing on home-based experiences of holidays and visits. They are drawing on their preoccupations with fantasy and imagination. Who knows where the dead chicken came from, but it clearly reflects a current personal preoccupation that creates a passive but participative role for another player who, at this point in time, has few opportunities for social interaction in school. What adult could identify a dead chicken theme as having potential to engage an elective mute child with her peers in social play?

Fostering friendships in young children

The 'whatever you want it to be place' brought a new dimension of friendship into the classroom, that of physical intimacy between young children. This was evident in these reception classrooms and, later, in the Year 1 classrooms. We observed cuddling and hugging. We observed children consoling and reassuring one another when play had been boisterous. We saw children initiating and taking on roles that had strong elements of nurture and stroking, such as 'being the baby' (an experience inevitably close in time given their ages) and 'being the dog'. Some further examples of this are given in the next chapter.

Alongside these affectionate and emotionally sustaining experiences, children also initiated and sustained themes that had elements of fear, danger and threat. Within their play, they found ways of confronting these elements together. Cooperative action brought the genie to slay the monster; a new direction ended the boisterous and potentially harmful roller coaster play with a suggested return to a quieter theme. In each case, the children were managing and controlling potential danger, whether imagined or real. As well as developing their coping strategies, they were cementing their friendships and perhaps also recognizing how shared interests can be personally rewarding.

Having reiterated the importance of allowing children opportunities to co-construct the curriculum, let us now look a little more closely at the role of the adult in the early years setting in promoting sociability and cooperation.

Chapter 4

Scaffolding the growth of sociability and cooperation

Children as co-constructors of the early years curriculum

This chapter draws together reflections on the role of the adult in assisting children's progress within and across the four domains of the Social Play Continuum. The previous chapters have illustrated the degree of sensitivity required by educators in responding to the nuances of children's language and action so as to understand fully the purposes, the flow, and the complexity of children's play. These chapters have also illustrated how interacting peers *need time in the classroom and access to flexible resources* to build momentum into their play, to develop reciprocity as they play, and to explore and develop together their emerging play themes as they draw upon their own experiences and interests. If we can give class-based and settings-based time, flexible resources and broad access to resources to young children, they take every advantage to co-construct their curricular experiences alongside the structuring provided by the educator. We begin to see how children's self-selected and self-directed activities take them quite naturally into the Areas of Learning of the Foundation Stage Curriculum in ways that are meaningful and challenging for them. As well as being meaningful and challenging, these experiences can consolidate and expand the children's growing understanding of the world around them – an essential condition for learning to occur.

None of this happens in a void; educators are there to assist children's progress. They do this in accordance with their own knowledge and understanding of what children need and in accordance with their expectations of children's capabilities – collectively and individually. As we have seen in Chapter 1, educators are also significantly and inevitably influenced by the prevailing climate surrounding curriculum development and by key messages that are emerging from related curriculum initiatives at any given point in time. Early years practitioners have a lot to think about and a lot to do.

Links with planning in early years settings

Chapter 1 has illustrated how these Areas of Provision (which now include the 'whatever you want it to be place') can connect with the Areas of Learning which comprise the Foundation Stage Curriculum. In part, this has been done so as to reassure educators that they are complying with current curriculum requirements while making these Areas of Provision available. These links can support their ongoing work in making more detailed connections during their own planning for play and learning in the early years. Fisher (2002) draws a useful distinction for educators in relation to planning. She advocates that:

- *long-term planning* concerns itself with a child's entitlement to a broad and balanced curriculum
- *medium-term planning* should then address continuity and progression from one stage to the next in the area of learning or the subject area
- *short-term planning* is then concerned with differentiation at the level of classes, groups and individuals and is directly informed through ongoing observation and assessment of children in action. Short-term planning aims to support the child's learning and progression.

Drawing parallels with Fisher's model and working within a context of promoting sociability and cooperation, the following framework may be helpful.

- *Long-term planning:* here, the practitioner is monitoring and planning for breadth and balance across the Foundation Stage Areas of Learning in conjunction with the Areas of Provision. These Areas of Provision have been identified by this research as important in relation to the growth of sociability and cooperation. There may of course be other Areas of Provision emerging within settings as also relevant, just as the 'whatever you want it to be place' emerged in this study. This research does not preclude the inclusion of other areas, but it has shown how these particular Areas of Provision lend themselves to the development of social and cooperative skills. It would not be assumed that everything is available to children all the time; only a few teaching–learning spaces might allow for this. It does seem important to monitor breadth and balance of provision over time, for the opportunities being made available to children for developing their social and cooperative repertoires.
- *Medium-term planning:* continuity of access to activities is so important if progression in learning and in the growth of cooperative skills is to be nurtured through access to Areas of Provision. It seems reasonable to argue that for some time now, because of prevailing circumstances, these Areas have been overlooked by practitioners when strategic review and development of provision has been made. However, this research has revealed how resources are used in different ways by different children, perhaps because of their individual competence, perhaps because of familiarity. Only by closely observing children's play can individual practitioners come to understand fully what this progression might look like within and across these Areas of Provision. It is perhaps also true to say that we need more research-based insights into progression in Areas of Provision. What this book is aiming to do is to offer some insights into how this progression looks in relation to the development of social and cooperative skills, and to offer the Continuum as a generic perspective on progression to relate to Areas of Provision and to inform the medium-term planning of learning opportunities.
- *Short-term planning:* it has been stated in the previous paragraph that observations can directly inform practitioner understanding in relation to decisions that are made in the medium term about how to support continuity and progression for children in the growth of their social and cooperative skills. Within the context of short-term planning for promoting cooperative skills development, the practitioner will be looking to scaffold the individual child's progression in the context of their interactions with other children. Observations will reveal individual need and strengths; planning and provision will meet those needs for individuals by providing

activities with interactive potential, and by assisting practitioners in making informed interventions and provision developments on a day-to-day basis.

Let us move on to focus a little more closely on issues of progression and scaffolding.

A brief look at Vygotsky

Lev Vygotsky died at the age of 37 in Russia, where he was born, and after only ten years or so of research activity. He was born in the same year as Piaget (1896) and, like Piaget, received no formal training in psychology. Vygotsky did not see the publication of his most important works or their influence on Western thinking, as this did not emerge until his work began to be translated from the late 1970s onwards. It is now widely recognized that much of his thinking may have been misrepresented in these early translations and that it may not even be wholly possible to translate some aspects of his theory. Vygotsky created an original theoretical system across his many Russian texts. As he did so, he also developed a terminology capable of expressing the new approach. In consequence, any translation runs the risk of distorting those ideas to some extent (Ivic,1994).

Nevertheless, there has been a very wide engagement by English-speaking writers with his works. Some of the key ideas of Vygotskyan theory do find expression in ways that have helped articulate and disseminate those key ideas. Some of these were quite visionary ideas on the early sociability of the child. In 1932, he wrote:

> It is through the mediation of others, through the mediation of the adult, that the child undertakes activities. Absolutely everything in the behaviour of the child is merged and rooted in social relations. Thus the child's relations with reality are from the start social relations, so that the newborn baby could be said to be, in the highest degree, a social being.
>
> (Ivic, 1994:473, translated from Vygotsky, 1982–84)

The social context for learning is a cornerstone of Vygotsky's work – hence its direct relevance to this publication. His works further our understanding of the use of cultural tools within that social context – spoken and written language are such tools and we use them, Vygotsky argues, to control and develop our own capacities for learning. We use physical tools also, instruments that we have invented and utilized to control the world around us. First of all, let us briefly put these ideas in the context of an early years learning environment and of this publication.

Children use the resources (tools) that are offered to them to change themselves internally. Their imaginative use of tools and artefacts is well recognized, for example when a construction block becomes a telephone or an empty plastic plate becomes 'dinner'. Wood and Attfield (1996) show how positively and easily interacting peers respond to the changing role of objects as a natural feature of their play. These resources become a crucial link between the child's internal developmental processes and the society or community around them – in this case, their peers and the adult educators. It is in using these resources for their own intent and purposes that they begin to co-construct the curriculum through their play; they take the context the adult has provided and shape it to their own ends and interests for whatever periods of time are available to them. As we have seen, in its earliest stages, they may do this through solitary or Associative Play (domain 1 on the Continuum). But, given the right conditions, this can progress to the more complex domains of Social, Highly Social and Cooperative engagement as they subsequently construct their curriculum, so as to better understand their society, in conjunction with their peers by learning how to combine their own ideas and use of resources (tools) with those of their peers.

Language is a means by which children share their thoughts and understandings. This is important for two reasons. Firstly, language consolidates their own developing understandings because its expression requires them to frame what they know internally (to process knowledge) and then to select words to express their understanding (to communicate knowledge). In communicating and sharing their understanding with those around them, young players are both informing others of what they know and also testing out their own knowledge base a little further by inviting a response. When we limit resource availability to young children (by that I mean the chance to use language at their own direction and limiting access to a range of learning materials), we run the risk of inhibiting this social–cognitive process. This is, in part, because we also limit their opportunities for using language in naturalistic ways to set and solve problems as they play and we limit the development of their play themes as an active means of exploring their own interests and experiences. One of the biggest threats that teachers involved in this research have expressed in relation to this has been the increased demand placed upon them to engage young children in formal, teacher-directed activities related to literacy and numeracy. It's a relatively simple equation. Too great a time on one thing means too little time for another. This is explored further in the next chapter.

Engaging with a teacher-led agenda rooted in formal teaching–learning experiences can sit quite successfully alongside a learner-led agenda rooted in play-based and self-selected activities, but issues of breadth and balance have to be engaged with – this is a job for the educator. Ideally, the educator engages in reflection on these matters with similarly engaged colleagues because the successful achievement of breadth and balance (the ultimate goal of long-term planning) is a complex and demanding task.

One of the ways in which Vygotsky's work differed from that of Piaget is that Vygotsky devoted considerable thought to the role of the educator in assisting children's progress. This is perhaps best expressed and most familiar to us through a consideration of his term 'zone of proximal development' (ZPD).

Vygotsky (1978:85–86) describes the ZPD as:

> The distance between the actual development level as determined by independent problem-solving and the level of potential development as determined through problem-solving under adult guidance or in collaboration with more capable peers.

The expert other (and this can be an adult or a child) assists the child to proceed ahead of development and to access adjacent domains within the learning experience (Broadhead, 2001). The ZPD is central within this work on children's sociability because the four domains of the Social and Cooperative Play Continuum are presented as actual zones of proximal development for supporting children's progression towards cooperation. As some of the early examples and discussion have illustrated, children's progress here is not a straightforward 'forward march' across the zones. Their progress can be impeded or enhanced by what adults say and do and by what the adults know, or what they think they know, about the intent and activity in children's observed play. Children's progress can be enhanced and impeded by levels of opportunity and by the range and potential of the available resources. Impact on progress across the zones of development within the Continuum can come from within and beyond the child; from her/his own inclinations and capabilities as well as from opportunities available to the child from within their teaching–learning environment.

The Continuum describes language and activity in the adjacent domains within the zone of proximal development that relate to the growth of sociability on into cooperation. As such, it is designed to be useful in better understanding children's play and how to support it through Areas of Provision. The Continuum is also intended to be useful in assessing the progress and needs of individual children as made evident in classrooms and other early years settings as they play. I say 'in classrooms' because we should never assume that children play as they do here when they are in other, non-institutional environments. Classrooms bring particular constraints and rules to children's play that may not be in force elsewhere. The Continuum can be useful in profiling an individual child's progress, and this is brought into focus again a little later in the chapter. First of all, let us consider some reservations about the purposes of assessment in relation to supporting children's progress and ongoing development.

Assessing children's progress as they play

In relation to ideas about the purposes of assessment and Vygotsky's work, Daniels (1993) has been critical of teaching activity that uses assessment activities to focus on what children *have achieved* rather than on *where they might progress with support*, i.e. on the summative rather than the formative. Drummond (2002:339) expresses this a little differently in her reflections. She talks about a need to 're-emphasize our understandings of *what* children are rather than *where* they are or what we *want* them to *have*' (emphasis in original). Both Daniels and Drummond are asking us to see the child within the context of their own development and of possibilities for future development rather than as having 'hit' preconceived, generic targets. It is a more fluid view of progression but in many ways is also more challenging for the educator. It is also these formative aspects that Vygotsky was striving to engage with in his own work. One reason that formative assessments are so challenging is that they (within the framework that Vygotsky was exploring) require the educator to keep more in mind than merely the next target. They ask the educator to understand and visualize a range of linked learning possibilities and to set these possibilities alongside context-related factors which may support or impede learning. In effect, the educator is being asked simultaneously to plan ahead while also recognizing the significance of the here and now in a child's development and progress.

In an early study of Key Stage 1 testing, Thumpston and Whitehead (1994:85) noted that assessment was being used for 'social control'. They went on to propose that 'a curriculum fit for children should do justice to the scope of their minds: wider forms of knowing are possible and evaluation must be able to capture such richness and diversity'. They conclude by remarking that play, risk-taking and experimentation are central to human development and learning. That's not to say, of course, that any of these opportunities will inevitably bring about learning; rather they can provide an environment that will optimize the possibilities for learning for young children.

Filer and Pollard (2000) in their studies in primary classrooms illustrate the pressures on teachers to formalize classroom assessment processes and the ways in which this obscures the richly complex realities of classroom life. Teachers become preoccupied with the content of the assessment rather than with the processes which surround and lead to the learning. As with Thumpston and Whitehead at an earlier point in time, Filer and Pollard also connect assessment in classrooms with forms of power and control by the teacher over children as s/he seeks evidence of summative achievement rather than insights into learning needs. In their concluding section, Filer and Pollard link the need for a broader perspective on assessment to the emerging insights that work on multiple intelligences is bringing (Gardner, 1983, 1993; Handy, 1997). The ongoing work on multiple intelligences is helping us to revisit ideas about the need for breadth and balance in curricular provision as we increasingly acknowledge that human intelligence can take many forms and that linguistic and numerate intelligence are only two of these. Handy (1997) identifies 11 intelligences:

- actual intelligence – can store and retrieve facts on a range of subjects
- analytic intelligence – to reason and conceptualise
- numerate intelligence
- linguistic intelligence
- spatial intelligence – to see patterns
- athletic intelligence
- intuitive intelligence – sensing what is not immediately obvious
- emotional intelligence – self-awareness, self-control, persistence and zeal
- practical intelligence
- interpersonal intelligence – getting things done with and through others
- musical intelligence.

It becomes apparent, when we consider some of the examples of play from previous chapters, how these multiple intelligences are simultaneously active as young children engage with other children in the different Areas of Provision. It might be argued that play is the most powerful forum for multiple, simultaneous engagement with the diverse forms of human intelligences that we currently acknowledge. Athey's work (1990) and Nutbrown's (1994) show how children's interests are revealed in their actions and their play. Children engage and re-engage with particular actions and ideas and, as they do so, they strengthen their intellectual schemata by making new connections to inform their developing understanding of the world and of their place within it. Some have argued that play is children's work, but I would say that it is far more than this. Play is their self-actualization, a holistic exploration of who and what they are and know and of who and what they might become.

Ownership of the learning process is a crucial motivating factor within an effective learning experience. The examples of children's play recorded in earlier chapters have illustrated ownership through their co-construction of the curriculum and their expressions of personal interests and experiences – when time is given to incorporate these into the daily activities of young children.

In the recent educational assessment climate, it has perhaps not been surprising that a focus on what children have achieved has prevailed – taking the form of the measurement of targets that are 'hit'. The climate of testing and league tables has generated a preoccupation with summative achievement and with preparing pupils to achieve well at certain points – namely age seven and age eleven. This in turn has fostered a climate whereby measurable achievement rather than opportunities for development has been important. That is not to say that educators have not engaged with ideas about the development of children's potential along a broader spectrum. However, the main preoccupations have been with the child's potential for completing and succeeding in formal literacy and numeracy tasks (as teacher comments earlier in the book have noted) rather than their potential to be socially and cooperatively active in problem-solving situations, their capacity for co-constructing the curriculum alongside the educator and their holistic need to nurture multiple intelligences. It is, perhaps, time to redress the balance.

Teacher assessment of pupil progress, across the curriculum and age range, remains a key issue. A later section in this chapter looks in some detail at how higher levels of opportunity for sociable and cooperative play have had a positive impact on children's behaviour in the classroom. These higher levels also had a positive impact in creating time for assessments, as Jane's following comments illustrate. She is arguing here that because of her redeveloped provision within a range of areas, the children's levels of independent activity, classroom confidence and peer interaction have grown. Consequently, she is able to focus on pupil assessments with her reception class, with fewer interruptions and greater concentration:

> Friday was a classic. I had three groups of children working on independent activities. I wanted to do some assessments. I had a teacher support working with a group on reading games. The three independent groups just did the task exactly as I wanted them. They put their equipment away when I wanted them to do it. They didn't come once to me saying they didn't know what to do. They sorted out their problems. I heard one girl saying: 'Matthew, you've got to roll that dice till it rolls properly', and he accepted that.

Before going on to look at how promoting sociability and cooperation are linked with positive approaches to behaviour management, let us have a look at some gender aspects of children's play.

Providing for boys and providing for girls – are their needs similar or different?

'Normal boys are naughty and playful, not violent. Normal girls are well-behaved, hard working and asexual.' In exploring these powerful and prevailing stereotypes of boys and girls, Walkerdine (1989, 1997) asks us to have a deeper engagement with the historical conventions that influence how we construct and understand 'childhood' and how we interpret and respond to boy/girl behaviours in modern society.

MacNaughton (2000) draws attention to two overriding factors which limit our gender possibilities. Firstly, that all Western cultures have dominant ideas about the correct way to be male or female, and secondly, that traditional and current gender order in Western cultures is patriarchal. I remember my son, Matthew, at about two years of age, playing with a toy iron off and on, all day, when visiting his cousin, Kerry. I bought a toy iron for home in which he took very little interest. His younger brother showed a very occasional interest in it. When Kerry came to us, she played for long periods with the boys and their cars. Her mother reported similarly that she showed little interest in such toys at home, although she had access to them. It may be that, despite our avowed intentions not to perceive 'boys and girls' toys, Kerry's mother and I unconsciously encouraged play with particular resources because of our own stereo-typed upbringing and its deep impact upon us. On the other hand, perhaps the children knew what they were interested in and, while novelty and associated interactions were stimulating for relatively brief periods, they were insufficient for extended engagement. Drawing on a range of writers in this area, MacNaughton (2000:143) comments that 'inequality will not disappear until we each desire and can choose to be male and female in different ways at different times'.

Jackson and Warin (2000) look at a number of research studies to support a view that it is between the ages of four and seven that children's understanding of the permanence of their gender group membership is laid down, and that this realization subsequently begins to affect the child's behaviour, especially regarding the choices of such things as toys, activities and playmates. They make reference to Davies (1987), who argues that by the age of three, we have learned the rules of presentation of self as male or female and how it is difficult – perhaps impossible – to unlearn these rules and to learn rules appropriate to the opposite gender. Perhaps this is what is happening to Kerry and my own two sons above, regardless of our 'motherly' attempts to stay gender-neutral. Perhaps our attempts were well-meaning but insignificant amid our own cultural baggage and societal expectations. I'm not suggesting that there's no point in trying to confront the stereotypes, but rather that we needed a better understanding of what we were trying to achieve and of the impact of the wider context in which we were trying to achieve it. In the conclusion to their paper, Jackson and Warin draw again from Davies (1987:56–57), who advises educators that 'children must be encouraged to find ways of signalling their maleness and femaleness without limiting or constricting their potential'. At this point it's worth pursuing these ideas a little further through a later publication by Jackson (2002), who reflects on the 'laddishness' of secondary school boys as a striving by them to retain and protect their self-worth in an era when notions of boys' underachievement are very strong in the media and in educational culture. It may be that boys begin at an early age to protect their self-worth (as do girls), that as the sense of self begins to emerge, the sense of separateness from the adult along with a growing sense of personal autonomy urges them to seek 'same as me' as crucial reference points for developing personal understanding. MacNaughton (2000) urges a 're-conceptualised gaze in early childhood' (p. 236) which includes:

- a multiracial feminist lens that brings into focus the intersections between gender, race, class, ability and sexuality
- a storyline lens that sharpens the focus on how children construct and experience gendered power relationships in their play with each other
- an ethics of the self lens that brings into sharper relief children's ways of transform-ing themselves into correctly gendered people
- a radical feminist lens that throws light on the positive attributes of femininity
- a masculinities lens that intensifies awareness of the different ways in which boys live and practice masculinities.

When I see this comprehensive list and read MacNaughton's well-structured arguments I understand why my purchase of the iron, and of other such toys, was well-intentioned but insufficient.

In further pursuit of understanding of gendered play and the growth of identity, let us look back at the gendered compositions of the scenarios that have been discussed so far. These are as follows.

School	Area of Provision	Domain	Gender composition and comment
Heartland	Home corner	Associative/ Social	3G/1B – little interaction across genders
Blue Grass	Small world	Highly Social	3B – interacting throughout
Long Deane	Water	Cooperative	3G – interacting throughout
St Andrew's	Sand	Cooperative	2B – interacting throughout
Royal Whittington	Large construction	Cooperative	1G/2B – from little to much cross-gender interaction
Royal Whittington	Sand	Cooperative/ Highly Social	3G/1B – interaction throughout with two other boys entering and leaving fairly quickly
St Andrew's	Whatever you want it to be place	Cooperative	3G/1B – interacting throughout
Burton Green	Whatever you want it to be place	Cooperative	2B/2G – interaction in gendered pairs and limited cross-gender interactions

The final scenario is the only one with a balanced, mixed-gender sample and during this play, the children tended to interact mainly in gendered pairs, occasionally sharing comments or ideas with one another across the gendered pairs (this was the play where Maria, an elective mute, was the 'dead chicken' for much of the time).

The composition of the above scenarios seemed typical of the observed play overall. Scenarios tended either to be same-gendered or to have a dominant gender with perhaps one player from the opposite sex. This has been an observable trend throughout observations in nursery, reception and Year 1; it is quite intriguing and perhaps partially explained by what is considered above in relation to how quickly identity might become established once the sense of self emerges. It seems that in these Areas of Provision, same-gendered pairs find much in common with one another in terms of shared play themes. Let's have a look at the overall figures across the 63 observations of the reception class research.

Boy only groups/pairs	Girl only groups/pairs	Mixed groups/pairs
14	14	35

This would suggest that in these classrooms, boys are just as likely as girls to want to play in single sex groups and pairs. Let us take the figure for mixed groups and pairs and break this down a little further.

Mixed genders with only one/two child(ren) of gender opposite to majority or with gendered groups in parallel play	Mixed genders, relatively even
20	15

Observations did reveal that there were some girls who seemed to regularly seek out opportunities to play in boy groups and boys who sought to play with girl groups, although I couldn't say from this research whether particular children *preferred* these kinds of groupings to any other kinds. But there was an observable trend across class-rooms which the teachers also noticed and commented upon.

In totalling these groupings, a tendency emerges for children to play either in single sex groupings or in mixed gendered groups where a minority (usually one, occasionally two in a larger grouping) of opposite-gender players are involved:

Single gender and minority opposite gender	Mixed genders, relatively even
48	15

This suggests that in these reception classrooms, while children were showing a preference for single-gender groupings when engaged in Areas of Provision, there are clearly children who enjoy participation in opposite-gender play and there are some examples (just under 25 per cent of the overall total) of occasions when children engaged in mixed gender play. The mixed gender play (15 observations) was spread fairly evenly across all Areas of Provision.

The next section presents and reflects on summaries of two scenarios that were observed in the same Year 1 classroom at Heartland Primary School. A focus on these two scenarios enables us to explore gender issues a little further.

Scenario 1: four girls are playing with farm animals

This play lasted for 35 minutes overall, with the four girls totally absorbed throughout. At one point, another girl tried to join them but was told that there weren't enough animals. She moved away to sit at a table, across from the boys described in the next scenario. The four girls have created enclosures using plastic fences and their cardigans. They sort the animals tidily into animal sets, making sure all the baby animals have a corresponding mummy. They keep the fierce animals from the gentle animals. Their play space is tidy and well-ordered; disarray is not tolerated for very long, their hand movements are very delicate and careful as animals are placed in close proximity. Their conversations are sporadic and about what the animals do and what they eat, about what the babies want and how the mummy will look after them: 'All these animals are very nice to one another'.

Scenario 2: two boys playing with jungle animals

The small world toys are spread around the table, fallen over, in some disarray. The boys select and use what they need at a particular point in time but do not arrange the materials in any special way. One remarks: 'My country is Africa'; the other: 'Mine is India'. They 'become' their animal of choice, making appropriate noises but also engaging in dialogue while in character. Sometimes the animals 'eat one another' with associated sound-effects and remarks about pain, blood, fear and dying. They move around the room, sometimes flying the vultures and making noises. They sit under the table together with animals for several minutes. It's difficult to hear their dialogue but it is constant and their body language and eye contact suggest deep absorption in their characters and play. Sometimes one will lean across the table to reach other animals/props and others will fall over; they are not rearranged. Things fall on the floor and are left there until needed.

When the girl who was sent away from the farm animals (Scenario 1) comes to the table, she watches for a short time and then sits and asks if she can play. The two boys look at each other and then sort and pass her a few animals. She negotiates a tree and plays with them in much the same way as the other girls were – in a very 'tidy' manner, arranging animals around the tree. She watches the boys play for much of the time.

At one point, one boy asks her if he can borrow her giraffe. He plays with it for a minute or two then returns it with a smile. After this, the two boys occasionally interact with her as they play together.

I remembered this girl from the research in the reception class the previous year; she was often observed playing with boys and the teacher remarked on her preference for male rather than female groupings at that time.

There are some clear contrasts in these two scenarios. My interest here is not in 'proving' anything in particular about how boys or girls may play – we couldn't prove anything with only two scenarios of this kind. Nor is it to claim that boys always play messily and with elements of 'violence' and girls always play tidily and 'caringly', but these are interesting aspects of their respective play styles to track in observation and to reflect upon. In fact much of the research into gendered aspects of play shows that these two scenarios are typical of the dominant characteristics of boy/girl play, but we need to avoid descent into stereotypical expectations from such a comment.

When they play in same-gender groups (and we have seen from the figures above that children may choose to do this quite frequently), girls' and boys' play may look very different but be just as valuable – both the scenarios described above were judged Highly Social, moving towards Cooperative, by myself and the class teacher. However, the nature of the play may have a different impact on adults. If females do have a greater preference for order in their environment than do males, then will female teachers welcome and value the apparent disarray sometimes evident when boys play in the same way as they might welcome the apparent control and order in that of the girls' play? And what should our goals be? We may think that the priority is to help the boys bring organization to the disarray, but might it also be to help the girls risk a little chaos in their lives? Herein might lay the benefits of actively encouraging cross-gendered play, of actively encouraging children to learn from one another, to move on from their personal comfort zones, however these have been engendered, into a less familiar play environment with new kinds of challenges.

It was also interesting to note that the boys' rather 'messy' play seemed more able to accommodate the entrance of another player. While the girl-only group prevented entry of a same-gender player, the boy pair accommodated the girl turned away by her female peers. Shifting a few pieces across to the new entrant did not disturb any carefully arranged scenes.

I continue to explore this coming together of 'apparent chaos' and 'order' in the next scenario, which focuses on the 'whatever you want it to be place' in the Year 1 classroom at Long Deane Primary School. Once again, there are interesting gendered aspects at work, on this occasion, in terms of how these children associate in same-gender grouping within a larger, mixed-gender group. Steve, the class teacher, had been very interested in the development of this Area of Provision when it had emerged in the adjoining reception class the year before. He now has the same children in Year 1 and has introduced the 'whatever you want it to be place' into the classroom.

On this occasion, I was videoing the children's play rather than observing it and using the Social Play Continuum to record, as had been my usual practice. Reflections on this play continued to illustrate, for me, how 'chaos' and 'order' are perhaps relative terms and how adult interpretations of play are essentially driven by adult interpretations of events.

This was a particularly humbling episode for me in terms of my own, still developing capacity to understand and value children's play, as will be illustrated in subsequent reflections.

Puppies, baths, toilets and washing machines

Five children had been playing in the 'whatever you want it to be place' for about 45 minutes and I videoed their activity throughout this period. I was a familiar figure to the children by this point and they seemed to take very little notice of me; the recording shows that there are only very occasional, relatively brief glances at the camera.

There are three girls and two boys in the area. The area is in a corner of the classroom; it is bounded on a third side by a storage area for the art area and partially bounded on the fourth side by an empty shop façade. It is a clearly designated area with very evident boundaries, providing quite a large space for play. The children have a small table in the centre of the area, several pieces of fabric, two cardboard boxes, a large plastic box, a role of newsprint paper (blank) and scissors, pencils, crayons. They have clipboards on one side surface and hats available but do not use these during this play.

First of all I am going to describe what repeated viewings of the video along with the children's commentary (I'll return to this a little later) have revealed to me about the flow of the play. Then I will share my own, initial feelings about the play, as experienced as I was filming and immediately afterwards. This was a key experience for me in two ways.

1   It forced me to recognize that despite many years of observing children at play, I remain subject at times to uninformed interpretations of play, especially when a video camera disengages me from direct observational contact with language and action in all its nuance and detail.
2   It has prompted me to want to take my own research further because the subsequent conversations with the players were so illuminating.

The scenario is described in the left-hand column. The right-hand column offers related information and my reflective questions to assist the reader in contextualizing the play.

Two girls (G1 and G2) are in the area along with two boys (B1 and B2) as videoing begins. G1 is wrapping a piece of silver fabric around herself, sarong-style and attempting to fasten it. This is proving difficult. A third girl (G3) enters. G1 remarks: 'You have to take your shoes off, take your shoes off'. G3 does so.

G3 asks G1: 'Can I be a dog? I want to be a dog.' G1 says yes.

G3 gets onto all fours and begins to bark.

Steve remarked later that the taking off of shoes was not 'his rule'; neither had it been decided upon in circle time discussions. It had emerged during previous play and was consistently applied by all the children.

Does G3 recognize and acknowledge G1 as being in some way 'in charge'? In fact G1 remains as 'the mother' throughout the play, continually tussling with her silver sarong but never giving it up – does the garment confirm her status in some way? Perhaps the garment is also important to sustaining the play theme, which is home-based, in that it clearly indicates that she is in character.

G2 announces that she wishes to be a dog but G1 says: 'No, we've got one'. G2 replies: 'You didn't ask me'. G1 ignores this and tells G2 she can be the baby. G2's facial expression suggests she's not too happy with this but there's no apparent dissent.

Somewhere in the play, G2 *does* become a dog; in fact she introduces a puppy theme that G3 also takes up. I'm not sure where the transition takes place but it is accomplished without any complaints from G1 in her role as 'mother'. Perhaps being a puppy is a compromise from being told to be the baby but wanting to be a dog.

B1 is sitting on a piece of fabric in one corner of the area. He alternately watches the girls, looks at the camera and stares ahead. He does not seem to say anything during this period, is quite still, but seems comfortable. After a time G3 comes across to him and speaks to him and waves her arms around. He laughs and imitates her gesture. She goes away. He watches her, laughing, for a while longer.

During this period, G1 'throws' an imaginary bone for G3 who 'catches it'. This theme is returned to and developed by G3 a little later in the play.

B2 wanders around the area for a similar period of time as B1 sits on the fabric. B2 also watches the girls occasionally, picks resources up and looks at them, very carefully.

B2 has been in the class for a short period only. He is Belgian and speaks English as a second language. Steve remarks that B2 has quite a wide English vocabulary but speaks quite slowly.

G1 is putting G2 and G3 (as puppies) into separate cardboard boxes and covering each of them with fabric. B1 and B2 watch this activity. They are silent and the three girls are conversing, in role. Gs 2 and 3 then get in a box together – a tight squeeze but possible. B2 speaks to Gs 2 and 3 but it isn't possible to hear what he is saying. They respond. He seems to point something out about Gs 2 and 3 to G1. She seems to respond to this.

The area is looking quite messy at this point, with discarded pieces of fabric scattered around. G1 retrieves some of them from the floor to cover Gs 2 and 3 in their boxes. As B2 walks around, he walks on the fabrics. The teacher in me inwardly winces.

continued on next page

B2 turns to talk to a boy who is outside the area. He has brought some Lego™ and bricks and is standing on the far side of the shop, using the empty shelf to rest the Lego™ on and construct. They chat together.

B1 remains sitting/staring/thinking (?) throughout this activity. B2 seems to be getting involved in the play but on the periphery rather than substantively with occasional conversation. This is difficult to hear.

G1 removes the roll of newsprint paper from the plastic box. She is saying something but it is not possible to hear what this is. B2 goes across to her and says something to her about the roll of paper. She sits on the roll of paper for a brief time, smiling.

G1 may be suggesting a new theme here which B2 might be reiterating. Alternatively, he may be suggesting another theme. As we shall see, the plastic box is about to become a 'bath' and the roll of paper is about to become a 'toilet' and then a 'washing machine'.

G3 has gone across to the boy with the Lego™ and placed a Lego™ board in her mouth. She gets down on all fours with it. G2 imitates this.

G3 gathers up the pieces of Lego™, the boy goes away. Several bits of Lego™ drop on the floor and are left there, occasionally being inadvertently kicked around as play progresses. I continue to wince inwardly; I have a strong need to suggest picking it up but remain in researcher mode and 'bite my tongue'.

G3 shows G2 the teeth marks she has made on the Lego™ board as she has had it in her mouth. G2 raises her eyebrows and smiles. G3 asks G1 to 'throw her bone'. G1 tosses the board a short distance onto the floor. G3 retrieves it and places it in her mouth.

B1 has risen from his seated position and has been walking around the area. He goes across to B2 at the roll of paper and words are exchanged. B1 imitates use of it as a toilet (standing) and B2 and he exchange smiles. B2 then sits on the roll and pulls a face and mimes a pushing motion. B2 has said that the plastic box is a bath. B1 climbs in, laughing, rubbing his arms and says: 'It's freezing'. B2 laughs also.

From his previously stationary position, we see B1 become integrated into the play quite rapidly. We also see the two boys playing together quite substantially from this point forward – their emergent play themes are pursued in tandem and while they do not exclude the girls, they mainly interact with one another while the girls continue to pursue the dogs/home themes.

B1 gets out of the bath again and stands at the 'toilet' again. Then he 'flushes' the toilet, laughing and discussing this with B2. He gets back in the 'bath' again. Then he gets out and stands at the 'toilet' again, miming its use.

B2 goes to G3, who is on all fours on the floor, and tries to take a piece of fabric from underneath her. She resists him. He says he wants it for the washing machine and goes to another piece of fabric. As he returns, G3 passes him the piece he originally wanted. They exchange smiles. He goes and pushes pieces of fabric into the washing machine and he and B2 smile and discuss. G1 comes over, there's some discussion with the two boys and she also pushes fabric into the 'washing machine'.

At some point, the 'toilet' has become a 'washing machine'.

Once G3 understands why B1 wants the fabric, she seems happy to assist him. B1 seems too absorbed in the play to want to create an altercation for the required piece of fabric; he just goes elsewhere to find some.

B1 puts his face close to the hole in the 'washing machine' and then says something to G1. He repeats the action and she gently presses his head down and then smiles at him. B1 then puts his arms into the roll of paper. G1 and B2 imitate this action and there is some discussion and smiling. B1 puts his leg into the roll of paper. G1 and B2 are smiling at him.

I'm not sure if the roll of paper is a toilet or a washing machine at this point, nor what B1's theme is in putting his face (followed by arms) close to the opening. But it quickly becomes a clear focus for cooperation and shared pleasure across the three children (and it emerges from discussion – see below – that he is 'washing' himself).

G2 and G3 are lying on their backs with their feet up calling out 'belly tickle, belly tickle'. G3 is gently prodding G1 with her foot but G1 is engrossed with the boys.

G1 begins to wrap B1 in a piece of fabric, like her sarong. He allows her to 'dress' him, they discuss and smile.

Filming stops at this point.

I think that had I truly recognized the themes at work and the momentum that was building in the play, I would have continued to film the play. In fact, play finished (to tidy up for playtime) about five minutes after this.

As I finished filming, my most immediate feelings were ones of disappointment. I had no real sense of any of the above themes, largely because, as I came to realize later, it is virtually impossible to film activity and to understand it while filming. What I felt I'd been witnessing at this point was very messy, non-directed and limited play with much aimless wandering, throwing and chewing of Lego®, disarray of fabrics and general lack of coherence or of uniting themes. What I subsequently came to realize I was filming was the coming together of male–female interests and the interconnecting of femininities and masculinities. I now believe that the dressing of the boy in the piece of fabric, right at the end of filming, was a very significant act, a non-threatening opportunity for the boy to explore his femininity as he played and for the play to extend into a marriage and weddings theme – possibly a recent, real-life experience for one of the children.

As the children were tidying the room, I played the recording back on the mini-screen and tried to identify why I felt so disappointed and why the play seemed so purposeless to me. An obvious thought struck me: if I wanted to better understand the play, why not ask the children about it? I negotiated with Steve for the children (if they wished) to stay in at playtime and view the filmed material on the mini screen. I said to them that if they wanted to talk about what they were watching, they could do so but if they just wanted to watch, that was fine also.

This was the humbling experience. They knew just what was happening, and explained and commented unselfconsciously. I did not ask any questions but let them speak as they wished. They were fascinated with watching themselves – the recent events were clearly still alive for them, they became reimmersed quite quickly. Some spoke more readily than others but all of them spoke eventually and seemed to be reliving aspects of the play as they watched. They talked to one another about their roles and actions, and recognized the need to explain actions to me. These were the actions I had not understood, and so gradually they shed light on the 'bones', the 'bath', the 'toilet' and the 'washing machine'. Coherence, structure, intention and themes emerged from the blur for me; I could recognize the high levels of reciprocity and see the growing momentum. I wished I'd had a tape recorder but here is some of the discussion I managed to write down as the children watched.

G3: We were being puppies there, she's mummy. (*pointing to G1 on the screen*)

B2: And we were daddies. (*looking at B1 who is standing beside him, watching the screen*)

B1: We weren't two daddies. (*looks at B2 and emphasizes 'weren't'*)

B2: Well then I was the cousin who came to stay. (*B2 seems to be prepared to readjust as they watch together rather than argue the point*)

B2: Andrew (*he means B1*) is in the bath.

B1: (*laughing*) It's freezing. Then I had a bath again because the water stayed hot after I'd had a wee. (*laughing*)

B2: After the wedding, Andrew and Tracey (*G1 in the silver sarong*) had a bath together. (*This happened after filming ceased; I had not been aware of a wedding theme but think it may have begun when G1 was dressing B1 in the piece of fabric, just before I stopped filming*)

G3: Were you weeing in the bath? She (*G2 – a puppy*) was weeing in bed. Now, you're weeing in the toilet. (*as G2 gets out of the 'bath' and goes to the 'toilet'*)

G1: Now we're still washing. (*the toilet had become a washing machine*)

B1: I was washing my leg. (*putting his body parts into the 'washing machine'*)

G2: I wanted a belly scratch. (*on their backs with their feet in the air*)

G3: I was kicking her bottom because I wanted a belly scratch. (*she is prodding G1, who is with the two boys at the 'washing machine'*)

Some further reflections

1   I was very conscious that I had been responding negatively to the apparent 'messiness' of the play area, whereas for the children, this was immaterial; indeed in some ways the 'messiness' was integral to the play.

2   The two boys took longer than the three girls to identify and establish personally relevant play themes. Once established, they had a deep commitment to them and their themes became a source of integration for girl–boy interactions as G1 (the mother) came over to their washing machine/toilet.

3   G2 and G3 sustained and developed their puppy theme; B1 and B2 sustained their artefacts themes (baths, toilets and washing machines); G1 was the only girl to interface with the two sets of themes and was perhaps building momentum towards a greater interface through the 'marriage' theme, although I don't know which of the three players suggested this theme.

4   As the children watched their play and discussed what they were seeing, they were operating on several levels and using language for multiple purposes. They were commenting on events on film while connecting these viewed events with previous and forthcoming events that had happened or were to happen in their play; they were continuing to negotiate and renegotiate their roles within the play; they were recognizing connections within their play themes from this more distant viewing of their recent play; they were ascribing purpose and intent to their actions within the narrative of their play; they recognized and explained the relationships between the narrative, their characters and the props (resources) that they were using.

This was a salutary experience for me, and has led to a desire to better understand gendered interactions in play and to focus on this in ongoing research. If boys and girls do have, broadly speaking, different areas of emphasis in their interests, then it is understandable that they may choose to play in same-gendered groups, in free-play situations, if such situations are not frequently encountered. It may be that time is needed to facilitate a recognized interest in and then engagement with opposite-gender activity just as it began to emerge in the puppies, baths, toilets and washing machine scenario.

It may also be that educators need to sensitize themselves to gendered interests and to their potential for positive impact, as Amy's reflection on her observations of play in the home corner illustrates:

> Interestingly, the boys in the home corner have been observed to bring in lots of ideas. I am thinking of one who was going off to Africa and was packing his bags and dressing up in different ways in the clothes.

Moving on from gender issues, the next section looks at impact on children's behaviour as perceived by the reception and Year 1 teachers involved in the research.

Areas of Provision – a positive impact on behaviour management

Behaviour management is a key issue in both early years and primary classrooms. There have been growing concerns for a number of years that classroom behaviour is deteriorating. We have to ask ourselves why this might be – if, indeed, it is. It is unlikely to be due to a single factor, but this research would argue that contributing factors *are* the limited opportunities available to children to co-construct their curriculum alongside adults, paralleled by increasingly limited opportunities for meaningful peer interaction in classroom settings. Because of the top-down pressures explored in earlier chapters, I would argue that this is also applicable in nursery and pre-school settings as the changing educational climate has placed different kinds of emphasis in the training–education of practitioners.

Jordan and Le Metais (1997), researching 10–12 year olds, identified breakdowns in teacher–pupil relationships, and the pupils' perceptions of the curriculum as irrelevant, as key contributors to resulting difficulties with behaviour management for teachers. Relationships seem more likely to deteriorate when educators feel pressured to reach pre-specified targets such as those associated with end of Key Stage tests. Jordan and Le Metais (1997) also show, in keeping with MacMullin's (1994) work, how improvements in social skills reduce classroom misbehaviour for older children. The relevance of these findings to the current age group lies in the recognition that now, many younger children are asked to operate with the high levels of teacher-structure which have, in the past, been more traditionally associated with older children's classrooms. MacMullin points out that poor interpersonal skills and a lack of empathy with peers are characteristics that can extend into adult life. Looking back on the scenarios so far depicted in this book, it is possible to identify numerous instances of peer empathy, peer assistance and altruism. The final chapter returns to these themes in greater detail. Linking in with these reflections relating to older primary children, the head teachers associated with the reception class and Year 1 research (having gradually, through visiting the classrooms, become impressed with the high levels of cooperation and task absorption evidenced in the reception and Year 1 classrooms) began discussing at project meetings why it might be that they were not seeing these types of interaction in their Key Stage 2 classrooms. If younger children could operate in these ways, then why not older children also? On further reflection, the heads admitted that these older children seldom had opportunities to cooperate, in relation to their own interests, for any length of time in their upper Key Stage 1 and Key Stage 2 classes – the skills being engendered in the younger children were in danger of disappearing as children progressed through the school.

In the ongoing reflections with both the reception and the Year 1 teachers, I gradually became aware of continuing references by the teachers to their perceptions of changes in children's behaviour as our joint research had continued. Both the reception and the Year 1 teachers had made more regular opportunities available to the children for engagement with the Areas of Provision. In addition, they were also talking more to the class about 'cooperation' and 'helping one another'. In the Year 1 class from which the above two scenarios (farm animals and jungle animals) were taken, Jean, the teacher, called the once a week afternoon session 'working together time' and emphasized to the children that they could choose where they played and worked but that they should try to work with a friend and help others who were playing and working there. In a matter of three weeks or so, she had started to see the impact of this in the children's behaviour, language and activity. In her observations, she had heard the children resolving conflicts by saying: 'this is working together time'; she observed them talking about 'cooperating' and 'sharing'.

Reflecting back on the progress of Joanne, the girl in the scenarios above who had tried to join the girls in the farm play and then had joined the boys in the jungle play, Jean had remarked:

> Joanne has always found it hard to cooperate but now she's really coming out of her shell. She still wants to dominate but she's getting better.

Jean's use of the word 'dominate' is interesting. It seems that when Joanne plays with the girls, she regularly introduces themes that are rejected, to such an extent that the girls may call upon Jean to 'stop Joanne being bossy'. This is reminiscent of Joanne's experiences recounted in the previous section. As with Steve's Year 1 class above, Jean's current class had also been involved in the research as reception class children in the previous year, and I too had noted Joanne's difficulties in becoming accepted in girl-only play. I had also noted how often she did as she does here and joined the boys' play. I wondered if Joanne's apparent diminishing of the desire to 'dominate' might be because when she is playing with the boys, her thematic interests more frequently match theirs. This links in with MacNaughton's (2000) ideas, discussed in an earlier section, about choosing to be male or female in different ways at different times.

During paired observations, Jean had also remarked on a boy with a special needs statement as being:

> no trouble in the afternoons when we do 'working together' but still has problems in the morning when it's more structured. Here, he's getting on with others.

Jean maintains that each of these two children is learning to modify her/his behaviour. Each child is showing clear potential for sociable and cooperative interactions but clearly needs particular kinds of opportunities in which to express, use and develop these skills.

On returning to the reception teachers for post-project reflections, further comments about behavioural changes were forthcoming and it was interesting to note how these tended to be about boy behaviours rather than girl behaviours. Angela's post-project comments illustrate how the observations had helped her see more clearly and articulate to the head, as well as to myself, a recognized need for more large motor activities for the boys in particular:

> The project has increased my commitment to the principle of play and it's increased my desire for continuous access to outdoor play. There are boys in parti-cular who need more large movement development. We are hoping to get some funding to extend the outdoor play for reception children. I feel I am letting them down, especially those boys.

The school subsequently secured some funding and extended the outdoor play area.

In the next extract, Jane reflects on the opportunity she was able to take for a focused discussion with a group of children, a discussion aimed at helping them to modify their behaviour but without drawing attention directly to the very inappropriate behaviour of one boy in particular.

> There was one incident where I stopped the play and we all sat around together [Jane and the four children] to negotiate how we could develop the play. I really thought someone was going to get hurt on that occasion. They were throwing cloths [pieces of fabric] around. One of the children has severe emotional problems and I didn't want to take him out of the play but it couldn't continue as it was so we all talked together. I didn't talk about his behaviour as such but about the play. They came up with really good ideas about how to use the cloths and how they could help one another with the cloths and seemed to have a new direction when they went back to the play.

Perhaps Jane felt it was legitimate to take time to talk about play with a small group because the research had a high profile in the school at the time but, inevitably, she also did so because her professional judgement led her to believe that a direct admonishing of this boy would not help in the longer-term modification of his behaviour. In acting as she does, she helps the children generate positive ideas for play, she reinforces the construct of cooperation in their play and she leads the boy into a positive learning experience rather than a negative interaction with an adult.

In relation to behaviour management, Rose commented on how irritating she found it when people came into her classroom and made comments like: 'Well of course you can allow these children to play like this because you have such well-behaved children'. In her mind, what such comments revealed was their singular lack of knowledge about how hard she had worked and how much planning and thinking she had done to create and sustain her Areas of Provision. Rose had reorganized her classroom to accommodate more Areas of Provision; she observed them regularly and discussed their development with her teaching assistant; she talked to the children about their play and encouraged them to share ideas that they had developed in their play; they drew and painted pictures of themselves playing in the Areas and talked regularly about their activities. In her mind, this was nothing to do with having 'nice children' and everything to do with her developed professionalism.

The final section in this chapter draws together some of these ideas that teachers identified as enabling them to integrate Areas of Provision into their classrooms in effective ways.

Scaffolding sociability and cooperation – some practical activities and suggestions

Class discussions and class rules

- These take place most effectively when the teacher and the class are 'in the round', often called 'circle time'. This facilitates eye-to-eye contact by all participants. This is particularly important to young children, who like to look at a face when listening to a speaker to aid their concentration and focus.

- Use your own observations to inform the discussions; for example: 'I saw you helping . . .'; 'It was interesting that you decided to . . .'. This can prompt children far more effectively than very open comments like: 'Tell us what you have been doing today'.
- During class discussions, encourage the children to talk briefly in pairs about what and who they have been playing with. Older children will respond to requests such as: 'Share one good idea with your partner about playing in the sand/water/etc.', leading on to the sharing of these ideas with the class.
- Ask the children to think and talk about 'how someone has helped you while you were playing'; ask them to think and talk about 'why it might sometimes be difficult to share our resources'.
- Ask the children to think about how you might make an Area better: what other resources might be made available to them? Some of their suggestions will be viable, some may be over-ambitious, some of the suggested materials can probably be brought from home and this reinforces a sense of curriculum ownership.
- Some practitioners find it useful to reiterate class rules relating to Areas of Provision at whole class times. As we have seen, in this research some teachers abandoned rules after observing play in the classroom and allowed children to, for example, regulate themselves in terms of how many could play in the sand or water or block play.
- Practitioners may feel that they will find it helpful to have a 'numbers allowed in' rule in the early days of provision of a new Area. However, it is important to reassure children simultaneously (perhaps in class discussions) that everyone will have the chance to play. Young children become anxious that their 'turn' with a new and exciting opportunity might not come along. How are they to know that it won't disappear just as quickly as it might have appeared? Hence the equal value of helping them to *anticipate* a new Area of Provision also. Discuss with the children the opportunities that will be available to play, whether it will be all day every day for a while, or three afternoons a week or one afternoon a week. Let them see that there's a system for being fair.
- Observations have shown that the application of a class rule about 'how many are allowed in' often leads to altercations that diminish the cooperative potential of an activity, right across the age range from nursery to Year 1. This particular rule application seems quite regularly to draw children away from a focused engagement with the Area and with each other. It interrupts momentum building. Is it really necessary?

Intervening in play

- Try never to disturb a playing pair or group by intervening without having spent some time, even if relatively brief, in focused observation (not necessarily using the Continuum at such a time). Any intervention is a disruption because it breaks the flow of play. It is important to get as strong a sense of context as possible and to understand something about the theme in action and the roles being taken before becoming involved.
- If you intervene so as to modify behaviour, talk with the children about the Area, the resources and how they might be used, rather than about the inappropriate

behaviour; try and habitualize positive rather than negative discussions, discussions about actions and theme development rather than about behaviour.

- If children ask you to intervene to 'sort out' altercations, try to 'buy yourself' a little bit of observation time before you respond. Sometimes it's the complainants that are creating the difficulties and are 'getting in first' so as to manage your response. As with the previous point, if you decide to intervene 'by invitation' then a focus on the Area and its potential rather than the perceived 'problem' can encourage the children to extend an inclusion to children seeking entry to the play.

- Sometimes children seek to keep others out of an Area because they know there are insufficient resources for them to bring their own well-established themes to fruition and to accommodate newcomers. It is important to be sensitive to this aspect and to consider what this might mean for resource development within medium- or long-term planning.

Resources

- Link small world resources to familiar stories and ongoing topics where possible.
- Have a range of small world resources closely situated to water, sand and block play along with other resources perhaps more usually associated with an Area of Provision. This might mean investing in good storage units; it might mean some degree of classroom reorganization. Free access facilitates self-selection to expand emerging themes, build reciprocity and maintain momentum.
- Good resources are expensive but worth every penny; where necessary, think about sharing across classes and settings so as to build a good supply and to link shared resources to joint planning for access and availability. With systematic review and development, there will eventually be sufficient for each class/setting to have a good supply.
- A well-thought-out storage system enables children to learn how to 'tidy up' more efficiently and effectively and independently. Allow sufficient time for tidying if an Area is new to children, be specific in your instructions, model the tidying up for them – perhaps use it as a 'circle time' activity to help them get the hang of it all.
- If you plan to change the room around, talk to the children about your ideas at circle time, BEFORE you make the changes. Ask for their suggestions and ideas; let some of them help you move the furniture. These activities help the children understand more fully that this is *their* learning environment. Often, children think that the classroom and everything in it belongs to the adults.
- Beautiful pieces of fabric are relatively inexpensive and very versatile. The children will respond to designs such as shells, stars and moons and leaves and incorporate these into their play themes.
- A wide range of resources, if available, will be used by children in creative and imaginative ways across all Areas of Provision – shells, pine cones, sticks, stones, leaves, etc.
- Provide occasional 'treasure chests' and 'rummage boxes' for sand and water play and encourage the children to add to these. Such resources can prompt new themes as well as resourcing existing themes.

- Ensure that any visits out of school, or visitors' talks, can be replicated in an Area of Provision or in more than one Area of Provision, for deep immersion in new experiences.

The 'whatever you want it to be place'

- As the scenarios have illustrated so far, cardboard boxes and pieces of fabric, a wooden clothes horse, pegs and bulldog clips and whatever else comes to mind make this an Area of Provision that is not costly to resource.
- Enclosure play remained popular into the Year 1 classrooms. This was illustrated frequently by children climbing into small spaces and building dens, caves, tents, etc., and linking these activities to their ongoing play themes.
- This Area doesn't necessarily need a large play space but it should be as large as you can reasonably make available. Some practitioners temporarily dismantled role play areas to accommodate the 'whatever you want it to be place'.
- Several teachers remarked that they would not introduce this Area of Provision to a new class of children, rather they would prefer to 'build up to it over time'. This meant allowing children to become familiar with one another through social and cooperative play opportunities within other Areas of Provision first of all, and perhaps introducing this Area in terms 2 or 3. Ideally, an introduction in term 2 with a return to the Area for an extended period in term 3 might be productive. This could be addressed through long-, medium- and short-term planning.

Planning and timing

- It seems important to see each Area of Provision as always being able to benefit from being 'in focus' for a while, but not to plan in-depth focus and development across too many Areas of Provision at any one time.
- Locate the timing for focus in the *long-term plan*, linked perhaps to the available space in the room or in the adjoining corridors.
- Let the *medium-term plan* identify stages of development (perhaps trying out different resources or locations over half a term; identifying relevant aspects of learning that connect, for example ensuring different types of clocks are available in the home corner or the 'whatever you want it to be place' when working on 'time' in maths).
- Let the *short-term planning* identify the times when it might be possible to observe the children at play in the Area of Provision in focus, the times when circle-time discussions will focus on the Area and particular links with literacy and numeracy exposure (discussed in more detail in the next chapter).
- Plan for times when teaching assistants can observe and be sure to compare and discuss observations with a view to:
  - further developing the Area of Provision and associated resources
  - identifying and responding to individual needs and where necessary planning individual programmes
  - identifying discussion points for circle time.
- Although the first point in this subsection suggests in-depth focus and development to be in relation to only one or two Areas of Provision at a given time, this is not to suggest that all Areas of Provision could not be simultaneously available in a

setting. In many nurseries and pre-schools they *are* simultaneously available, for very good reasons. This guidance is suggesting that *active review and development* be limited to one or two Areas of Provision at any one time, as this will be linked to careful observation and related reflection. Careful observation needs dedicated time.

The next chapter continues to examine how the curriculum can be co-constructed by children and adults, and brings literacy and numeracy more firmly into the debate.

Chapter 5

Literacy and numeracy

Harnessing emerging interests and skills and continuing to co-construct the curriculum

A conversation overheard between two girls in a reception class in the 'whatever you want it to be place':

Girl 1: I'm a princess. (*swirling her flowing 'gown' around her ankles*)
Girl 2: We're playing Robin Hood.
Girl 1: Oh!
Girl 2: You could be Maid Marion.
Girl 1: Is she a princess?
Girl 2: No, (*pauses*) but she's very beautiful,
Girl 1: Alright, I'll be Maid Marion.

In this short extract are expressed empathy, negotiation, information and bonding – plus a link with recent literacy experiences.

Chapter 1 offered a detailed overview of developments in the educational world from the mid-1980s onwards. This was to illustrate how these developments had impacted on early years provision and how so many of these areas of impact were ultimately quite negative for reception aged children in particular. Amid these substantial changes were, in the late 1990s, the introduction of the Literacy and Numeracy Strategies, what Craft (2002:134) describes as 'formalized, compulsory, highly structured teaching outlines', and what she sees as representing a shift away from the conception of an early years teacher 'as a professional artist'.

Many reception teachers found themselves in something of a cleft stick during this period towards the end of the old and into the new century as far as the literacy and numeracy hours were concerned. Nationally, LEAs varied quite considerably in the ways in which they addressed the issue of the literacy and numeracy hours for reception children. Lacking clear guidance from government on this age group, anticipating the potentially heavy hand of Ofsted, and especially in those parts of the country that lacked a clear steer from experienced, confident and articulate early years advisers (an increasingly rare breed), reception children found themselves 'doing' the literacy and numeracy hours either by default or by design. As Chapter 1 detailed, heads were engaged with their governors in target setting for end of Key Stage 2 test scores with the LEAs, who had *their* targets set for them by the DfES, everyone having been 'geared up' to meet the national targets set by David Blunkett when Minister for Education. We know now that the targets could not be met, with 73 rather than the prescribed 75 per cent meeting the maths target at Level 4 of the National Curriculum and 75 rather than 80 per cent meeting the English Level 4 targets in 2002.

Along with the LEAs, heads and governors were also anticipating Ofsted inspection with an associated inspection schedule that offered little support in making judgements about young children's real dispositions for learning (Dowling, 2000). At the end of this long chain of target setting sat the reception children, lost from sight for a long time as a growing belief took hold that the sooner we got them started on 'formal learning', the better they would perform in their end of Key Stage tests. In many cases, this view impacted on nursery settings also (Miller, 2001). I did some professional development work with early years teachers very recently where a nursery teacher remarked that 'We do more formal things in the morning because the head wants us to get them ready for school, but we *do* play in the afternoon'. A prejudice has taken hold, rooted in panic and ignorance rather than in informed action in many LEAs and schools during what Anning (1995) has referred to as the turbulent years for Key Stage 1 teachers.

Reception children (and some nursery children) across the country became subject to various formats of the respective 'hours' taking up substantial parts of each school day and, to greater or lesser degrees, closing off access to the Areas of Provision once traditionally provided in their classrooms. Parents also had a voice here, as Wood and Attfield (1996:9) note, as they became increasingly resistant to seeing 'play' in the classroom and pressed to see children 'doing the National Curriculum'.

Back in the late 1980s (DES, 1989), Her Majesty's Inspectorate (HMI; Ofsted's much-respected predecessors) had published their inspection review, which had focused on the education of young children. This document began by setting out some underlying principles, which included: 'purposeful play features strongly' (para. 16). The document goes on to reiterate nine areas of learning (DES, 1985), subsequently presented as six curriculum areas and including mathematical learning and experience, and language and literacy. These areas of focus are presented, along with the remaining four, within a context of the exemplification of good practice and a particular need to give attention, at this point in time, to the curriculum for young children with the 'introduction of the National Curriculum' (p. 3). Early years educators were increasingly dismayed at how little status was given to play as the National Curriculum emerged (Wood and Attfield, 1996) and how the essential character of children's learning in the primary phase had been ignored by the introduction of a subject-based curriculum (Siraj-Blatchford, 1993). It was to be another 11 years before educators would receive a curriculum designed for young children – in the Curriculum Guidance for the Foundation Stage (QCA, 2000). There has undoubtedly been a legacy from these years of neglect, and we ignore it at our peril in looking to implement the Foundation Stage Curriculum and its related assessments. Dowling (2000) draws attention to concerns that the Early Learning Goals would label children as failures at five. Despite having waited for so long, we should not be too ready to presume that the Foundation Stage Curriculum is the panacea we need. While, as Craft (2002) states, it may be bringing play resources back into the reception classroom, she also remarks (Craft, 2000) that there has been an increased time-share and emphasis on formal learning resulting from the literacy and numeracy hours as a result of these national strategies and their impact on early years classrooms.

Given the burden of pressure over time from government, Ofsted, LEA, head, governor, colleagues and parents, how might the early years educator be supported in defending the potential that Areas of Provision have for promoting learning in relation to mathematics and language and literacy *and equally*, what might be the inherent dangers in justifying Areas of Provision as a means of promoting literacy and numeracy?

Co-constructing literacy and numeracy learning

Linking observations with small group discussions

This chapter opened with a conversation recorded between two girls. Here is communication, language and literacy – speaking and listening connected to reading experiences – at their most powerful yet contained in a brief exchange between two peers. In this small cameo they combine their worlds, their interests, their experiences through negotiated exchange.

The present section offers a longer exchange between me, Ben, Michael and Scott, three very young reception children whom I had observed playing with the Duplo™ just prior to this discussion. Our conversation lasted only four minutes, yet they demonstrate so much because they are reflecting back on something that they have experienced so intensely – rather like the Year 1 children as they watched the video with me in the previous chapter. These three boys are physically active throughout this chat. They stand and sit, lay on the table and twirl around occasionally. Young children, perhaps more especially boys, speak with their whole bodies until another mode is acquired. But in between the movement is some interesting reflection along with a casual determination to manage me and to ensure that playtime isn't missed.

In the right-hand column some related assessment targets in the FSP are identified (Foundation Stage Profile; QCA, 2003). The number reflects the section in 'Language for communication and thinking in the FSP' (page 19 onwards). Along with these assessment-related targets are also identified some rather more sophisticated uses of language that are present here, but not represented in the FSP – *indicated in italics*. Scott is a boy with perceived behavioural difficulties; he has trouble sitting still for formal learning activities – note his 'excited' and quite profound response below.

There are two purposes for using this example:

1   to illustrate how detailed observations of children's play can provide a meaningful context for brief discussions – discussions that give evidence of learning and provide a context for promoting learning
2   to remind ourselves that children's thinking and understanding are a challenge to access because their language is still in development and because adults' perceptions of intent are only ever partial. Their language may be in development, but their thinking is powerful and creative.

Pat: Ben, tell me what you've made. Tell me what you've made.

I am trying to attract and hold Ben's attention.

Ben: A racing car.

Pat: And what else?

Ben: An alligator in water.

1. Ben listens and responds.

Pat: And where did you get your ideas from for these models?

This is a complex question.

Ben: I just made 'em.

Ben's response is factual and perhaps gives him some thinking time for an answer to this complex question.

Pat: But where did the idea come from?

6. Interacts with others . . . taking turns in conversation.

Scott: (*excitedly*) I know, I know right, we can remember to make some toys at work and then we can play with them.

I think Scott is combining his worlds here; he is recognizing that ideas can be transferred from one context to another; he is excited because he has an answer to a difficult question and because he recognizes an internal state of 'knowing'.

Pat: So you can make what you want?

Ben: Yeah.

Ben agrees; perhaps Scott's answer takes his own understanding a little further.

Pat: Ben, you know when you're playing . . .

Ben (*interrupts Pat*) What's that? (*and points*)

7. Uses talk to clarify events.

Pat: It's just a tape recorder. You know when you're playing with your toys; you sometimes use different voices, don't you? Sometimes you use an ordinary voice and sometimes you use another voice.

Michael: Well that's what we were doing.

6. Interacts with others . . . taking turns in conversation.

Pat: Why do you use a different voice, it's ever so interesting?

Michael: 'Cos we want to.

8. Speaks clearly with confidence and control, showing awareness of listener.

Pat: What does it help you to do when you use a different voice?

Michael: It helps you make imaginations.

9. Talks and listens confidently and with control, consistently showing awareness of the listener by including relevant detail. Uses language to work out and clarify ideas, showing control of an appropriate range of vocabulary. *Like Scott above, Michael is thinking beyond the event; he is understanding and communicating at a complex level.*

Pat: It helps you make imaginations? So when you use a different voice are you sometimes a different person?

Michael: Yeah, I've got, I've got, Ben and me and we've got another friend Lee, he plays with us.

Michael seeks to clarify through further examples. Perhaps in his mind, he is recalling another time of 'different voice use'.

Ben: Mousies can't talk can they, they can't talk? (*I think talking mousies are linked with 'imaginations'*)

9. Talks and listens confidently and with control, consistently showing awareness of the listener by including relevant detail. Uses language to work out and clarify ideas, showing control of an appropriate range of vocabulary. *Ben is recalling previous thoughts and experiences that relate to this discussion.*

Pat: Only in your imagination.

Ben: If you do that with your finger and bang it, it comes out (is talking about a piece of Duplo™).

It is impossible to know whether or not this is a continuation of the 'mousie' conversation.

Pat: Why does it do that?

continued on next page

Ben: I do it.

Pat: Why?

Ben: 'Cos it doesn't hurt. I get another piece and put it in.

Pat: Oh. When you sat down to play with your Duplo™ did you know what you were going to make or do ideas come later?

Michael: We just maked, maked them.

Pat: But did you know what you were going to make?

Ben: We're going to miss playtime.

Pat: It's alright, we've nearly finished. Did you know when you sat down what you were going to make?

Michael: Right (*very firmly*) he were, right, I was going to make a motor car, he was going to make a racing car and I was going to make a robot.

Pat: You didn't want to do anything to do with the farm?

Scott: I said, shall we make a robot Michael?

Pat: Aaah! You said that and what did Michael say, can you remember?

Scott: He didn't make a robot.

Ben corrects my interpretation of events, he is literal and precise – unlike my comment.

6. Interacts with others in a variety of contexts, negotiating plans and taking turns in conversation.

7. Uses talk to organize, sequence and clarify thinking.

Ben provides essential information to influence my activity; he is asking me to consider his immediate needs.

8. Speaks clearly with confidence and control, showing awareness of Listener. *I think he is seeking to summarise the discussion and to draw it to a close.*

The Duplo™ was a farm set with animals, fences and buildings.

9. Recalls relevant past events and communicates with precision. *My farm comment is ignored, quite legitimately as it is not relevant to the ongoing discussion.*

Michael: I didn't want to. These two were robots.

Scott: This one can change into a monkey.

Pat: So you can change it if you want to.

Scott: We can change them over, each others and put them like that and we've finished them.

6. Although they are each speaking very quickly at this point, they are taking turns in conversation.

5. Uses language to imagine and recreate roles and experiences.

Ben: He says no and he says yes.

Pat: So yours is talking?

1. All three boys can listen and respond.

Michael: It's playtime now.

They are standing up at this point, eager to go out to play.

8. Speaks clearly with confidence and control, showing awareness of listener. *Michael perhaps recalls Ben's earlier comments and determines that the conversation is finished at this point – and why not? He manages me firmly and with clarity and courtesy.*

. . . And on to Key Stage 1

As previously noted, the research project had expanded in the five schools into the Year 1 classrooms. Here the teachers agreed to continue making Areas of Provision available, although not necessarily all Areas of Provision simultaneously. However, some provision and paired observations continued and, as with the reception teachers, the Year 1 teachers began to identify and reflect upon the opportunities that became available to children to connect their learning from teacher-directed tasks with their play in the Areas of Provision – the kind of activity exemplified by the opening conversation in this chapter. These older children were more sophisticated in their ideas for their play and they also used the available resources in more complex ways than the younger children had. They could connect ideas and experiences more rapidly, it seemed, as they played. The pace was faster on occasions (although not always), the language was more complex and the cooperation was built around a more rapid exchange of ideas and of problem setting and solving similar to the examples that Beardsley (with Harnett, 1998) reproduces. In addition, their role play was beginning to take on clearly apparent dramatic qualities. Hutt *et al.* (1989) showed how children's language is more complex in pretend play than in non-pretend interactions; dramatic conventions are emerging in their play and might be further nurtured, as Hendy and Toon (2001) point out, through planned interventions by the adult.

The Year 1 teachers provided literacy and numeracy materials around the Areas of Provision. The reception teachers had also resourced the play, to some extent, in this way, but it seemed more commonplace in the Year 1 classrooms. In part, this may have been because the Year 1 teachers were *very* concerned about 'fitting in the research' around their literacy and numeracy hours. It seemed more alien to them than it had to the reception teachers to provide open-ended and flexible play resources. So they may have provided the related resources to quell their fears about the possible 'neglect' of numeracy and literacy. However, we were subsequently able to observe how readily and easily the children incorporated the reading/writing and mathematical materials into their play. In doing so, we could also see how the children used these objects, just as they had others, as tools for further constructing and extending their own developing knowledge-base alongside their preoccupying play themes. The literacy and numeracy artefacts had similar potential for building momentum and reciprocity as had all the other resources we had studied.

The following extract comes from June's classroom at Royal Whittington Primary School. She has already been introduced, having been one of the two reception teachers previously involved in the research. By this point, she was a Year 1 teacher, with the same group of children and looking to build on the cooperative skills she had seen them develop in the previous year but in an age-appropriate way and with the National Curriculum in mind. In this extract, which is summarized for discussion purposes, the children interface literacy and numeracy activities throughout their ongoing play. This illustrates how these are not discrete learning activities for children.

June had introduced the 'whatever you want it to be place' into the Year 1 classroom and referred to it by this name in her discussions with the children. She had resourced the area with a table and chairs, a telephone, clipboards, small whiteboards and felt tips/cloths, pencils and scissors, hats, a clock, some story books. Plates and cups were close by on shelves. She had had two discussions with the children at circle time about the area. From these discussions had come a list of words concerning what the area could be used for. These were the children's ideas, and included Burger King™ and McDonalds™. During her previous observations of the play (June remarked that the children never approached her when she was observing these days; they were quite used to her in this role), the area had been a train and a bus. On this occasion it was a school. The following offers a summary of our joint observations, highlighting some key aspects.

- The school theme lasted throughout the play but it ebbed and flowed around a dog/puppy theme and a washing clothes theme (interestingly, identical themes to those seen when video recording in Steve's classroom).
- One boy muttered to himself for a few minutes 'on the sidelines', which I noted as 'self talk'. However, when he returned to the play he said he was 'the head teacher' and had clearly been 'getting himself in character'. He then, still 'in character', went and found the class jotters of the children in the area, gave them out and 'did some number work' with the children, who participated quite happily for several minutes. He collected the jotters and returned them to their place in the classroom. He remained in role throughout this time and, impressively, caught many of the head teacher's characteristics.

- One girl, in role as the teacher, fetched reading cards and showed them to a boy. She read the word, he repeated it, both totally absorbed at a level that suited their respective, but different, reading abilities.
- McKenzie, a solitary player, watched this girl and boy for some time without actively participating, but who knows what was being processed (see below)?
- One girl fetches some numbers and she and another girl play at finding odd and even numbers – this had featured in their numeracy tasks during the week. One becomes the teacher and one the pupil, and the play continues. Sometimes mistakes are made, but usually one of the pair recognizes and corrects the mistakes.
- The same two girls made continued use of the whiteboards, writing letters and numbers, sharing and commenting and then beginning to write stories, all while being 'in character at school'.
- One girl seems to be a leader; she fetched pieces of fabric into the area but did not use them immediately. She also fetches an abacus into the area and 'demonstrates' how it is used to a small group of assembled children. About ten minutes after fetching the fabric, she begins to spread it on the floor – perhaps a new theme is emerging – but then tidy-up time is announced.
- The play was not dynamic; rather it was a continuing series of gentle interactions across a boy pair and a girl pair with the four occasionally coming together. My notes remark at one point: 'An intense cosiness and helpfulness exists across the group, a quiet intimacy'. The mathematical features of the play were substantial, with children rehearsing and practising activities that June said had featured in their numeracy work during recent days.
- McKenzie (diagnosed with severe developmental delay) took some numbers away from a girl, who was not pleased but did not seek adult help. McKenzie looked at the numbers for several minutes, giving then value (some were correct, most were incorrect). When he had finished he returned them to the girl, with a smile, and she and he sat together looking at the numbers. She corrected his mistakes; McKenzie repeated her words and smiled at her. June remarked afterwards that this was a substantial development for him in several ways – recognizing another child's needs, interacting with another child in his mathematical learning, taking an extended interest in numbers and their value. The observation had allowed June to note important progress and had allowed McKenzie to demonstrate his newly emerging social skills and his emerging mathematical knowledge.

Developing the Area of Provision in the Year 1 classroom

- A main challenge for June at this time was how to make the designated space look like an Area of Provision. She was rather concerned that it always seemed to look messy, although she valued the activities that were undertaken in the Area. She was trying to find ways of helping the children to see the space as a *designated* play space with clear purposes with which they could identify.
- The Area was labelled, as were some of the shelves, to support children's tidying activity and to communicate to other adults that there was a guiding plan and underpinning principles for this space. June was also beginning to discuss the Area with the teacher support assistant, as June had realized that uninformed adults also tended to treat the space as a 'dumping ground'.

- June has a flip chart on the wall, where she noted some of what she has observed in the Area. She then used her observations and these notes to frame and inform her discussions with the children at circle time to share their ideas and expand their knowledge-base. She also reiterated the importance of cooperation at these class discussion times by remarking on some of the helping behaviours she had seen, and invited the children to talk about who had helped them and whom they had helped.
- June had mixed feelings about using the Area as the basis of a group activity in the literacy and/or numeracy periods. While she didn't doubt its potential for contributing to literacy and numeracy development, June did not want to be prescriptive about the Area. She wanted the children to continue to value it as a place in their classroom where their ideas and experiences were important and could find voice in ways that they determined.

June is right to be guided by her reservations, just as I am being very careful here not to claim that play can automatically promote literacy and numeracy. Roskos and Christie (2001:80) drawing on Johnson *et al.*'s (1999) work, explore play as a self-help tool 'that allows children to achieve higher levels of cognitive functioning'. Like my own work, Roskos and Christie draw substantially on Vygotsky's theory relating to the zone of proximal development, quoting from Vygotsky (1976:552), who argues that: 'in play, a child is always above his average age, above his daily behaviour; in play, it is as though he were a head taller than himself'. I think it is these qualities that June is also noting as she observes the children's play, and McKenzie's responses perhaps illustrate this also.

Specific links can be made between children's play in Areas of Provision and opportunities to develop mathematical learning and communication, language and literacy as articulated in the Foundation Stage Curriculum, the Foundation Stage Profile and the National Curriculum. These potential links have been addressed, although it was clearly never an aim for this research to become a means of delivering a centrally determined curriculum. It would not be too difficult to extrapolate from these examples to look more substantially at how particular kinds of resources and objects, once located in or near an Area of Provision, might also enhance such opportunities.

Roskos and Christie (2001) believe from their own work that play *can* serve literacy (and, from my extrapolation, numeracy) in a similar way, i.e. 'by providing connections between oral and written modes of expression' (p. 59). However, they also have reservations, underpinned most substantially by 'concerns about definitions, theories, methodology, lack of progress in establishing causal connections with development and dominance of the "play as progress" rhetoric'. Vygotsky (1962:98) has something to add at this point:

> Written speech is a separate linguistic function, differing from oral speech in both structure and mode of thinking. Even its minimal development requires a high level of abstraction. It is speech in thought and image only, lacking the musical, expressive, intonational qualities of oral speech.

Taking Roskos and Christie's last point, we cannot 'prove' progression in any of the above episodes. However, we can reiterate the centrality of the oral culture for children of this age and see something of the connections between language, objects (tools) and manifestations of thought and understanding. Egan's (1988) work has also emphasized the young child's intellectual and emotional need to engage with oral cultures and the centrality of fantasy as a prominent part of their mental lives. Vygotsky (1962) also notes that young children have little or no motivation to learn writing. The child feels no need for it, and has only a vague idea of its usefulness. Young children's oral culture can only live in the classroom if the adults around them will give it space and status, just as June seeks to do above. As we saw also from June's classroom, when the children see a meaning for writing – to communicate within their play – they will choose to draw upon and so deepen the skills and knowledge communicated to them, by expert others, at other times.

Marsh (1999, 2000) illustrates this in a literacy context with her studies of young children's super-hero play in classrooms – an attractive proposition, she finds, for both boys and girls, despite other views that girls may prefer weaker characters. As well as challenging a few stereotypes, the girls and boys in her small study were intellectually and emotionally engaged with their super-hero discourses and were simultaneously engaged with literacy activities within their role play. While the boys explored functional uses of literacy, the girls would often use writing as a means of expression (Marsh, 1999). All of them incorporated powerful oral narratives as they conjoined a world they knew well from beyond the classroom with the literary demands of their Key Stage 1 classrooms. Miller (2001) has described the Curriculum Guidance for the Foundation Stage as a 'more optimistic document' (p. 114) because it recognizes the role of play in early learning and offers the opportunity to 'shape a more learner centred literacy curriculum'. While I welcome and recognize this optimism, I still believe that shaping the learner-centred literacy curriculum remains a profound challenge for us in terms of enabling children to combine their worlds and simultaneously co-construct the early years curriculum.

Similarly, 'meaningful mathematics' is by no means a new construct. McNamara (1995) points out how children can complete pages of sums without any real understanding and also (1996) how skills developed at home and in nursery settings may become lost when more formal mathematics experiences prevail, because the skills acquired at home are no longer seen as high status – by the teacher and, subsequently, by the child. Mathematics is a traditionally difficult subject for many teachers, and personal feelings can impact on subject knowledge and on pedagogical subject knowledge (Aubrey, 1996; Stephen and Wilkinson, 1999). Thinking laterally while feeling uncertain makes substantial demands on adults; watching children in their play can deepen professional knowledge about how children learn mathematical concepts and how they connect mathematical ideas; this in turn can inform effective teaching in powerful ways.

Taking all this into consideration, how might learning in literacy and numeracy, in their broadest forms, be complemented by Areas of Provision being made and developed in early years classrooms? This final section in this chapter draws together some concluding thoughts. While these aim to inform practice in practical ways, they are not intended as prescriptions of good practice but rather as further points for reflection.

Literacy and numeracy – returning to Areas of Provision

Sand and water play

- Focused observations will reveal the mathematical constructs that children identify and engage with in relation to the resources available.
- Focused observations will reveal the imaginative and oral links that connect the children with their experience of the literary world, whether through books or other media.
- Different resources (objects/tools) will be associated with different language/constructs at different points in time. While we cannot predict the constructs that will connect with the child's interests and knowledge at a given point in time, if variety is available, the child can select and utilize as the ideas are formed and developed (evident in their play themes).
- Peer interaction, reciprocity and momentum will fuel the emerging themes and associated mathematical constructs. While their respective experiences outside the classroom may or may not have something in common, their mathematical experiences from teacher-directed activity inside the classroom will provide common ground – even though individual children may understand this common ground at different levels.
- The adult's role is to provide variety in resources; this is linked to their personal knowledge of the relationships between the resources and the understanding they can promote.
- Storage and access are key features for sand and water play, and will support or constrain the child's developing understandings. What the adult provides and how the adult regulates access are key pedagogical issues that can be most substantially informed by detailed observations and reflections on learning links. Watching the children play leads to informed decisions about locating resources which in turn lead to more effective pedagogy informed by insights into learning.

Construction and small world

- Find ways to share these resources across classes if necessary; they are expensive but so intellectually and emotionally engaging for children – and so versatile.
- Focused observations will reveal the mathematical constructs that children identify in relation to the resources available.
- Focused observations will reveal the imaginative and oral links that connect the children with their experience of the literary world, whether through books or other media.
- Allowing children to access resources class-wide will enable them to deepen their play themes, to deepen their intellectual commitment to the activity, and will immerse them in their oral culture and their associated design quests. Such a flexible use of resources and their management requires circle time discussions as well as some strategic thinking and planning by the adults in the classroom.
- Children might talk together to plan their designs before their physical activity starts.

- Children might record their finished designs through drawing and writing in books that they make in a nearby writing area.
- Children can photograph and print their completed designs and add text in class books.

Role play – predetermined (e.g. the home corner) and open-ended (the 'whatever you want it to be place')

- Focused observations can alert adults to children's interests, experiences, pre-occupations and concerns. Emotional experiences must 'find voice' in the classroom if children are to truly see this as *their* environment in every sense.
- Marsh's work (1999, 2000) urges practitioners to be alert to children's TV and cinema experiences as legitimate manifestations of their literary experiences. Give these experiences status in the classroom through teacher-designed (a specified play area perhaps) and through pupil-themed imaginative play.
- Provide objects and artefacts within play areas that resonate with current and previous mathematical experiences: clocks, the abacus, number cards, clipboards, individual whiteboards, etc. Ask the children to think about what they would like to take into the Area. Have games around for easy access. Encourage them to see the whole classroom as a resource for their play and learning.
- Encourage children to find ways of recording their play experiences and activities – writing, talking, photographs (let the children take them), filming.
- From your observations, note down their play themes, share these themes with the children in conversation and at circle time, and talk to the children about how their play activity and interests might become drama and script-writing (Hendy and Toon, 2001).

In the coming years, we might hope to see the literacy and the numeracy 'hours' with their associated high levels of teacher direction disappearing from reception class-rooms and, correspondingly, open-ended play-based activities, balanced with adult-structured inputs, replacing them. Clearly that is to be welcomed and, as the extracts above have reiterated, literacy and numeracy learning need not disappear with them but can remain integral if:

- related resources are available for pupils to incorporate spontaneously into their play themes
- adults recognize how adult-directed activity, in small doses, will be re-engaged with, by pupils, in their free choice activities.

Getting this right might come to mean that literacy and numeracy skills and knowledge can be taught and learned through a co-constructed curriculum in our early years classrooms and settings.

Chapter 6

Emotional well-being, making choices, time to learn

Life is too hard, say children aged four

Four-year-olds suffer depression

The first headline is taken from an article in *The Times* (14 June 1999) by Alexandra Frean, who went on to report that 'the rat race is starting earlier than ever'. It draws on a study by Jacqui Cousins entitled 'Listening to four-year-olds' in which children talked of being 'too hurried to play'. One girl reported that she had to work hard and not play so she could get ready 'to pass my Key Stage 1 tests'. We have looked in previous chapters at the effects of this prevailing climate.

The second quote is from a BBC news website dated 8 March 2000 (http://news. bbc.co.uk) The Mental Health Foundation states that an increasing number of children, some as young as four, are being diagnosed with depression. The director, Ruth Lesirge, is quoted as saying:

> We know that mental health problems in children are on the increase. We also know through our work in school and community projects, that work to pro- mote the good mental health of children and young people is effective. We are talking about some quite simple things that help children to develop networks of friends, increase their self esteem and give them the skills, confidence and ability to relate to a wide variety of children and adults . . . We are not neces- sarily talking about children being diagnosed with serious illnesses. But we are talking about being aware of the risk factors that might lead to a child develop- ing mental health problems.

Among these key factors, she identifies 'less freedom to play, isolation and inability to make relationships with other children and adults'.

Promoting emotional well-being for young children in early years settings

Chapter 4 looked at multiple intelligences in relation to assessing children's learning and made a claim, relating to young learners, that: 'Play is their self-actualization, a holistic exploration of who and what they are and know and of who and what they might become'. This manifests itself most substantially, I believe, when children operate within the Cooperative domain. Play in this domain combines visual, auditory and kinaesthetic learning opportunities. It gives children crucial thinking time through joint problem setting and solving. The more cooperative the play, the more likely it is that children will connect with and understand other children's knowledge along with a deeply fulfilling, emotional engagement with the world around them. Sociable and cooperative endeavours expose children to other children's perspectives and as such they become experts for one another, scaffolding their own and their friends' learning experiences. These endeavours are also a crucial source of knowledge for adults in deepening their own understanding of the world of play and of how they can scaffold appropriately and effectively within that world.

Goleman's work (1998) has focused a great deal of much-needed attention on one of these multiple intelligences – emotional intelligence. It is now widely acknowledged that to function effectively in our increasingly complex society we need to actively manage our interactions with others. These are the issues that Jacqui Cousins and Ruth Lesirge are addressing above. When children are able to operate within the Cooperative domain and, I would argue, when they play with others who manage this domain effectively even if an individual may not do so her/himself, they are operating within a state of emotional intelligence.

In conjunction with a growing awareness of the need to broaden our understanding of intelligence within human development has come a better understanding of how motivation is linked with well-being. A simple example here is access to water. Thirsty children do not learn well (neither do thirsty adults, but we can generally work out when we will get access and motivate ourselves accordingly). In recognition of this, many schools have repaired their water fountains or provided access to water in the classroom. This is a well-being issue. Dehydration limits concentration and diminishes the likelihood of the child being in a 'learning state'. Children often don't realize they are thirsty; they fidget or disrupt their peers, displacing their feelings of discomfort but unable to name them. Or in fact they've learned not to ask if they can go for a drink because their teacher may associate such a request with a non-legitimate 'time-out opportunity'. We are starting to more explicitly recognize and thus to act upon the connections between well-being, motivation and learning by providing water for children. I would ask for the same in terms of emotional well-being.

The next part of this final chapter explores these issues with a focus on two scenarios. In doing so, it aims to draw on a broader context of factors influencing children's good mental health and emotional well-being, and of how practitioners might support this in their classrooms given also the prevailing constraints of some effects from policy-making, as explored in previous chapters.

Little sadness, big sadness – needing friends and needing help

I listened in to a conversation in a school staffroom. Researchers have a tendency to do this as a matter of course, I'm afraid. This was not one of the research schools. The conversation related to two children, one of whom had remained in nursery (Karl) and the other of whom had moved into the reception class (Lee). Karl and Lee had been great friends in nursery; their mothers were also friends and each mother had spoken separately to the respective teachers about the impact of the separation on her son. Clearly the mothers were concerned and no doubt discussed their concerns in front of the two boys, a natural activity. I had picked up this background information, having spent the morning in nursery. The nursery teacher had communicated this background information to me and also remarked at how pleased she was that Karl had settled well and seemed not to be missing his friend. It was her comment on this that led to the staffroom discussion when we went in for coffee. After the nursery teacher had shared with her colleagues that Karl seemed settled, the reception teacher remarked: 'Lee fell over at playtime and started crying. He said to me: "The reason I'm crying so much is because I miss my friend in nursery".' This may have been an echo of his mother's discussions; nevertheless, he was, quite reasonably, associating his unhappiness with a need for his friend and, wherever this came from – from his own internal perceptions or from his conversations with his mother, or from hearing her chat to her friend – it was clearly a powerful need at that moment.

The reception teacher reported that she had said to Lee 'Oh there's no point thinking about that'. A second reception teacher immediately contributed: 'They've got to move on'. I don't think the nursery teacher agreed with their perspectives. She said nothing, but her face looked a little troubled. I felt troubled. In their busy teaching lives, the two reception teachers seemed to have lost sight of the importance of friendship for Lee and Karl. There was a sense of the need to 'toughen up' in this tough world communicated by their unreflective and spontaneous responses to this incident. This prevailing view does not mean they are unfeeling. I am not accusing the two reception teachers of neglect or emotional abuse of young children, by any means. But the incident prompted me to wonder where the caring that I am sure still formed a part of their 'being' as a teacher was hiding, and why it was not able to illuminate their understanding of children's needs. Friends are important to us. They are a necessary part of our stability and emotional well-being. They share our achievements and our concerns, our joys and sorrows. Young children also have these feelings – of course they do, we know this.

As we become older, we 'consign' our friendships to certain parts of our lives. We create a range of social opportunities to sustain and extend our friendships depending on our individual needs and inclinations. Young children do not separate friendship from ongoing daily activity, although they may associate different friends with different contexts. They are building their concept of 'friend' just as they are building their concepts of so many aspects of daily life that adults take for granted. When children ask: 'Are you my friend?' or say: 'I'm not your friend any more', they are checking out the boundaries of friendship, testing their understanding of the construct, deepening their knowledge of the social structures that govern all our lives.

Their routines and, with them, their access to their friends, are largely determined by the adults around them. The kinds of activities they can engage in with their friends, and for how long, are also controlled by adults. In structuring their learning opportunities, including play, the adults are also influencing the emerging constructs of friendship and the extent to which an individual child feels able to determine and develop those friendships and social relationships within their wider world.

In fact, Lee and Karl could have quite easily accessed one another at this time of Lee's 'little sadness'. The school had recently redesigned its outdoor play area to allow for reception and nursery children to play together. This development was underpinned by a philosophy of protection and nurturing of young children's play opportunities as befits their early years status. Lee and Karl could have been brought together quite easily for a hug or a chat.

The reception teachers' responses to Lee's needs may, to some extent, be explained by the extended, prevailing climate outlined in Chapter 1. Such contexts shape knowledge and action for practitioners and might actively inhibit the growth of understanding about children's needs and inherent links with learning. Adults' knowledge and action are also quite clearly informed by perspectives on gender and societal expectations, as discussed in Chapter 4.

In many of our classrooms, despite the levels of professionalism and caring, there is not enough time to care about and to better understand the emotional life of the young child. This kind of understanding is what underpins the philosophies and pedagogy of the kindergarten provision in the Reggio Emilia area of Italy. Howard Gardner remarks in the foreword to Edwards *et al.* (1998): 'In Reggio, the teachers know how to listen to children, how to allow them to take the initiative, and yet how to guide them in productive ways' (p. xvii).

The practitioners in the Reggio Emilia nurseries have had 40 years of thinking in these ways to underpin their actions; they see themselves as learning about learning and how to support it and engage in this as a continual and very active process through reflective debate with colleagues. New practitioners are trained and educated into the underpinning philosophies; they are 'bathed' in these ideas as they train and when they work. Professional discourses about children's activities and how they can be supported are an integral and continuing part of planning, observing and assessing children's needs. Cathleen Smith reports on a conversation with Ivana Soncini, a psychologist– *pedagogista*, specializing in special education in the area. Soncini remarks:

> We take a lot of care with all of the children's feelings. Especially for children who have special rights, we have to give them credit for their feelings and pay attention for ways for them to learn to express themselves. Sometimes people get so focused on cognitive skills that they miss the children's feelings. Feelings are important for everyone; and kindness and sensitivity to others need to be supported in all the children.
>
> (Smith, 1998:208)

The two reception teachers discussing Lee and Karl were quite young women; the nursery teacher had more years of experience. There is a training/maturity issue here, clearly recognized in the Reggio approach to teaching and learning for young children about guiding practitioners towards a deeper understanding of how emotional equilibrium is linked with motivation and learning for young children, and also, how it is linked with quality of life experiences as the sense of self becomes shaped, affirmed and sometimes, unfortunately, immutable.

There is a word of caution to be sounded here, however. As Moss (2001:125) notes: 'We cannot escape responsibility for making our own choices about early childhood by "buying in to a Reggio programme".' Moss explores what can be gained by reflecting on the Reggio model and what the implications are for us in relation to our own developing philosophies and underpinning rationales as we make and develop our provision for young children in our own political, economic and social context.

I referred to Lee's 'little sadness' above, but many young children carry much greater burdens of sadness in their young lives, born of their social contexts and economic circumstances in the family. Through their substantial investment in the Sure Start programme and through the sustained expansion of childcare places, the current Labour government have recognized the extent to which poverty can undermine and restrict a child's educational progress. At the turn of the century, statistics were revealing substantial numbers of children living in poverty in the United Kingdom: more than four million, which is 1 in 3 children (Rahman *et al.*, 2001). The current government programme seeks to offer expanded childcare opportunities as a way of supporting parents, predominantly lone parents within the government agenda, back into education and work as a means of moving out of poverty. Lone parents are more likely to be living with poverty. The Rahman *et al.* report also shows that the number of homeless households living in temporary accommodation has doubled since 1997 and that more than half of these households have dependent children. Their findings lead them to conclude that successive generations of children may be learning to be poor. These economic factors clearly impact on the quality of life in families, and also inevitably impact on quality of life experiences for young children. Of course, not all practitioners will be providing for children who are living with poverty, but these statistics show us that the numbers may be far greater than might be realized.

The following section on classroom observations at Heartland Primary School illustrates a somewhat greater sadness than that of Lee above, although this is not to belittle Lee's unhappiness and need for friendship. This example is also concerned, in part, with friendship as we see how play in the home corner brings out the altruism and persistent concern of one friend for another.

It also seems important to offer this illustration in defence of the home corner. In Chapter 3, the tabulated findings had shown role play areas as least likely to stimulate play in the Cooperative domain. This had led to discussions among the project group from which the 'whatever you want it to be place' had emerged. Despite this, it is important to recognize the valuable contribution that role play can offer young children in engaging with the familiar in playful *and* intellectual ways. I wouldn't want anyone to take a message from this book that role play has little or nothing to offer young children.

Cohen (1993:4), in a list of quotations from a range of people, includes one from Piaget dated 1951 that states: *We can be sure that all happenings, pleasant or unpleasant in the child's life, will have repercussions on her dolls.* Allowing for the replacing of her with her/his, to reflect current attitudes and values on non-sexist play, this comment retains some resonance in relation to allowing children outlets and opportunities for coming to terms with their own emotional experiences, as can be seen in the forthcoming section.

The section also returns reflection in this final chapter to the 'teacher as researcher' issues explored in Chapter 3. This book has endeavoured to make a strong case for encouraging early years practitioners to see the value of informed and regular observations of learning from a research-based perspective and to encourage practitioners to adopt research-based strategies within their provision. It has been acknowledged that this requires a substantial culture shift for practitioners and for their own learning/

professional development experiences, and that this brings a particular set of associated challenges that cannot be ignored.

A central premise here is that it is only when we start to see something of the complexity of children's play that we really begin to understand the vastness of their learning. The final sentence from this quotation from Barrie Thorne (1993:12) was used in Chapter 3; at this point, let us take a look at the broader quotation:

> To learn from children, adults have to challenge the deep assumption that they already know what children are like, both because as former children, adults have been there, and because, as adults, they regard children as less complete versions of themselves. When adults seek to learn about and from children, the challenge is to take the closely familiar and render it strange.

Heartland Primary School – the home corner

Rose and I sat together to watch three girls in the home corner. It is clear from the entries on the Continuum why we subsequently determined that this play was pre-dominantly within the Social domain. Of the three girls, one is making a cake and another (Emily, the focus of this extract) is stuffing dolls in a cupboard. The third girl, Sophie, is a friend of Emily's; they play together a lot. Rose provided this information in our post-observation reflections after we had both come to understand the extent of Emily's unhappiness. We had also by this time understood the persistence that Sophie had shown as she had tried to initiate an interaction with Emily; Sophie seemed puzzled by the lack of response from Emily and had subsequently persisted in trying to make contact with her. It seemed that Sophie was actively grappling with Emily's apparent unhappiness and seeking to help her friend through it.

Let us look at the Continuum first of all. Following on from that, further observational notes associated with the numerical entries will be used to illustrate Rose's, mine and Sophie's growing awareness that Emily was possibly deeply unhappy.

Faulkener and Miell (1993) show in their work how children work better when paired with a friend than with an acquaintance – their existing interpersonal relationships will be an important factor in collaborative learning.

The Social Play Continuum – Side 1: a tool for play observation, pupil assessment and evaluation of Areas of Provision

| Observation start time: **1.45pm** | Children entering play: **GGG** | Observation finish time: **2.00pm** |
| Area of provision: **Home Corner** | Children leaving play: | |

L = Language   *A = Action observed*   *L/A = Language and Action combined*
RL = Reciprocal language   *RA = Reciprocal Action*   *RL/RA = Reciprocal language and reciprocal action combined*

ASSOCIATIVE DOMAIN

A: Looks towards peers
A: Watches play
A: Imitates play **1, 11**
A: Object offered, not accepted **34**
A/L: Object taken, altercation **21, 29**
A: Parallel play period
L: Self-talk **4, 8, 20, 27**
A/L: Comment on action directed at peer; peer does not respond **10**

SOCIAL DOMAIN

A: Smiling **31**
A: Laughter **2**
L: Play noises, play voice
RA: Eye contact made
A: Object taken, no altercation **32**
RA: Object offered and received
L/A: Consent sought and object accessed
L: Approval sought, not given
RL: Approval sought and given
L: Instruction given, no response **3, 23, 24**
L/RA: Instruction given, positive response
L: Question asked, no response **22, 38**
RL: Question asked, response given **30**
L/RA: Comment on own action/ described intent directed at peer, peer looks **6, 7, 9, 13, 25, 33**
RL: Comment on own action/ described intent directed at peer, verbal response **5, 12, 14, 15**

HIGHLY SOCIAL DOMAIN

RA: Offering/accepting of objects evident
RL: Dialogue, a mix of activity related and non-related but a theme is evident
RL: Comment on own action/ described intent with acknowledgement leading to extended exchange **16, 26**
RL: Sporadic dialogue develops role play themes **17, 18, 35**
RA/L: Eye contact/laughter (play noise) combined as behavioural cluster **19**
RA/RL: Brief reciprocal sequences, e.g. giving/following instructions, seeking/giving approval, offering/accepting objects, asking/answering questions **28**
RL/RA: New ideas or resources have impact on developing theme

COOPERATIVE DOMAIN

RA: Offering/accepting objects sustains/extends play theme
RL: Sustained dialogue is activity related and clear theme(s) emerge
RL: Explanations/descriptions utilized
RL/RA: New idea/resource extends play and is sustained
RL/RA: Children display a shared understanding of goals
RL: Offering and accepting verbal help
RA: Offering and accepting physical help **37**
RL/RA: Verbal and physical help combined
RL/RA: Problem identified and solved
RL/RA: Sustained dramatic scenarios enacted linked to play theme(s)

Emergent play themes noted: Cake making, setting table, stuffing dolls in cupboard and putting 'roughly' to bed

Emily and Sophie – a friend at work; emotional intelligence in action

Points 4, 8, 20 and 27: at each of these points, Emily is putting dolls into a cupboard and shutting the doors while muttering to herself. It's not possible to hear what she is saying. The tone of voice, the look on her face (angry) and her bodily posture (rigid) suggest strong emotion at work.

At points 9 and 10, Sophie, who has watched Emily putting dolls in the cupboard, declares her intention to do the same (*point 9*). Emily looks at Sophie and, perhaps encouraged by this point of contact, Sophie repeats her intention but Emily ignores her (*point 10*). Sophie imitates Emily's action (*point 11*) but Emily seems too engrossed in her own activity and inward reflections to make any further contact with Sophie. Sophie seems to think Emily is playing a game, and has not yet understood that Emily is unhappy. Emily doesn't connect with Sophie because she isn't playing a game; she's engaged with her inner turmoil.

At point 12, Sophie shows her doll to Emily and says: 'She's crying as well'. Emily replies very forcefully 'She isn't'. By *point 28*, there has been a dialogue between Sophie and Emily but, as we see from the following, this interaction cannot be sustained by Emily without periods of altercation.

At points 21 and 29, Emily takes first a doll and then a plate from Sophie. At *point 29*, Sophie is clearly upset and pleads to Rose to help her. Rose does intervene, as we are both aware by this point of Emily's distress and of how it is affecting Sophie. It almost seemed in Sophie's plea to Rose that she was asking for more than the return of a plate; she wanted the return of her friend and wanted Rose to help her. Sophie's distress and puzzlement were clear. Emily returns the plate to the table as Rose comes forward to intervene and Rose praises Emily.

At point 32 Emily again takes a plate from Sophie who is laying the table. Sophie watches but does not object. She looks at Emily as if she is thinking deeply about the meaning behind these actions. It was as if the taking of the object was Emily reaching out for contact with Sophie and that Sophie was perhaps beginning to form an understanding of this.

At point 33, Sophie has put on a dress from the dressing-up rack; Emily has a similar dress on. Sophie remarks to Emily 'I am a beautiful princess'.

At 35, Emily allows herself to be led across to the bed by Sophie, who is saying to Emily that if she goes for a lie down she will feel better. Emily lies on the bed and then gets up again quickly to move a few dolls around in their cupboards. Sophie goes across to Emily and says with genuine enthusiasm and for the first time, a little happiness in her voice: 'You look *wonderful* with that dress on', putting strong emphasis on 'wonderful'. Emily doesn't smile but she holds Sophie's gaze for several seconds.

Post-observation reflections

- Rose felt that the observations needed to be acted upon on Emily's behalf. She had thought as she watched that it might have been appropriate to take Emily away from the play to discuss her feelings with her and to allow the other two girls to play without being interrupted by Emily. However, on reflection she felt that allowing Emily to continue was beneficial because of the bond that emerged with Sophie. Hindsight had shown that Emily's need for friendship and assistance was greater than either of the others' needs for uninterrupted play at that point in time.

- Rose reflected on some changes in the domestic arrangements in Emily's home during this period. Emily's mother had told Rose about the changes, perhaps because she recognized that they were having an impact on Emily's behaviour at home. Until the period of observation, Rose had not actively connected the conversation with Mum with changes in Emily's behaviour in school. The 15-minute observation helped Rose to make connections with a previously rather vague notion about Emily being different at school, the conversation with Mum and the need for immediate action on Emily's behalf. She resolved to have another chat with Mum and to find an opportunity to chat with Emily and with Sophie, separately.

- Both Rose and I were surprised at the levels of sensitivity and sophistication that Sophie had demonstrated as her own understanding of Emily's needs had grown – we had both learned something new about the complexity of response that a young child might be capable of. Sophie's intuition seemed strong as she strove for helpful behaviours amid her own uncertainty and unhappiness. There were clear gains for her as well as for Emily in allowing Sophie the chance to extend her own repertoire of helping behaviours in an emotionally charged encounter.

One of the claims I have made for this research is an advocacy of the 'whatever you want it to be place' as able to make a very important contribution within young children's learning. The research claims that it is, to quite a significant degree, the open-endedness and flexibility in the associated resources of the 'whatever you want it to be place' that allows children to manipulate them in accordance with their own experiences, interests and continued explorations of self-identity. Consequently themes emerge which are sustained and elaborated as play continues. There has also been some discussion in Chapter 4 of how high levels of open-endedness and flexibility in resources create and sustain opportunities for connections across masculinities and femininities as momentum builds, reciprocities develop and play themes start to interconnect.

For girls and boys the challenge as Moss (2001:129) reports, is 'to offer a context in which the child can themselves explore and go deeper into a problem'. Not only does play offer this crucial context; play offers opportunities for emotional exploration and expression, opportunities to make and strengthen friendships, opportunities for deepening language skills and, perhaps most of all, the chance to take ownership of learning, to construct understandings and, in facilitative early years environments, the chance for adults and children to co-construct the early years curriculum. While play belongs to children, its facilitation offers a bridge for adults into the child's thinking and understanding.

There's a need for a cautionary note at this point, it seems. The preceding chapters have illustrated how Areas of Provision can deliver the Foundation Stage Curriculum and how observations and discussions with children can provide evidence towards Foundation Stage Profiling. However, play is important for far more than its capacity to deliver a government's agenda for young children's learning and it would be devastating if the next or even this generation of early years educators came to believe that this was the purpose of play. Achieving the Early Learning Goals is only a tiny part of what play offers children; let's not forget that.

Perhaps it is now time to shift the emphasis in the early years; time to move from a position whereby starting with the child has prevailed into one where we begin from an informed understanding of learning. As we move into an era where observation in early years settings should become the norm rather than the exception, let's not think about watching the children; rather let us think and talk about understanding their learning.

References

Anning, A. (ed.) (1995) *A National Curriculum for the Early Years*, Buckingham: Open University Press.

Anning, A. (1997) *The First Years at School*, Buckingham: Open University Press.

Athey, C. (1990) *Extending Thought in Young Children*, London: Paul Chapman Publishing.

Aubrey, C. (1996) 'The nature of teaching mathematics subject matter in reception classrooms', in P. Broadhead (ed.) *Researching the Early Years Continuum*, Clevedon: Multilingual Matters, pp. 128–150.

Balageur, I., Mestres, J. and Penn, H. (undated) *Quality in Services for Young Children*, London: European Commission Childcare Network.

Beardsley, G. (with Harnett, P.) (1998) *Exploring Play in the Primary Classroom*, London: David Fulton Publishers.

Bennett, N. and Kell, J. (1989) *A Good Start? Four Year Olds in School*, Oxford: Blackwell.

Bennett, N., Wood, L. and Rogers, S. (1997) *Teaching through Play: Teachers' Thinking and Classroom Practice*, Buckingham: Open University Press.

Blurton-Jones, N. (1967) 'An ethological study of some aspects of social behaviour in children in nursery school', in D. Morris (ed.) *Primate Ethology*, London: Weidenfeld & Nicolson.

Blurton-Jones, N. (1972) *Ethological Studies of Child Behaviour*, Cambridge: Cambridge University Press.

Brierley, J. (1993) *Growth in Children*, London: Cassell.

Broadhead, P. (1989) 'Working together towards a better understanding of the primary classroom', in P. Lomax (ed.) *The Management of Change*, Clevedon: Multilingual Matters, pp. 130–146.

Broadhead, P. (1995a) *Researching the Early Years Continuum*, Clevedon: Multilingual Matters.

Broadhead, P. (1995b) 'Changing practice; feeling good – primary professional development explored', *Cambridge Journal of Education*, **25**, 3, 315–326.

Broadhead, P. (1997) 'Promoting sociability and co-operation in nursery settings', *British Educational Research Journal*, **23**, 4, 513–531.

Broadhead, P. (2001) 'Investigating sociability and cooperation in four and five year olds in reception class settings', *International Journal of Early Years Education*, **9**, 1, 24–35.

Broadhead, P., Cuckle, P. and Hodgson, J. (1999) 'Promoting pupil learning within a school development framework', *Research Papers in Education*, **14**, 3, 275–294.

Broadhead, P., Cuckle, P., Hodgson, J. and Dunford, J. (1996) 'Improving primary schools through school development planning – building a vision; exploring the reality', *Educational Management and Administration*, **23**, 4, 277–290.

Broadhead, P., Hodgson, P., Cuckle, P. and Dunford, J. (1998) 'School development planning in the primary school; moving from the amorphous to the dimensional and making it your own', *Research Papers in Education*, **13**, 1, 3–18.

CACE (Central Advisory Council for England) (1967) *Children and Their Primary Schools*, Plowden Report, London: HMSO.

Carr, W. and Kemmis, K. (1986) *Becoming Critical*, Lewes: Falmer Press.

Case, P., Case, S. and Catling, S. (2000) 'Please show you're working: a critical assessment of the impact of Ofsted inspection on primary teachers', *British Journal of Sociology of Education*, **21**, 2, 605–621.

Charlesworth, R. and Hartup, W.W. (1967) 'Positive social reinforcement in the nursery social peer group', *Child Development*, **38**, 93–102.

Chorpita, B.F. and Barlow, D.H. (1998) 'The development of anxiety: the role of control in the early environment', *Psychological Bulletin*, **124**, 3–21.

Cleave, S. and Brown, S. (1991) *Early to School. Four Year Olds in Infant Classes*, Windsor: NFER-Nelson.

Cohen, D. (1993) *The Development of Play*, 2nd edn, London: Routledge.

Cosaro, W.A. (1985) *Friendship and Peer Culture in the Early Years*, Norwood, NJ: Ablex Publishing Corporation.

Craft, A. (2000) *Creativity Across the Primary Curriculum*, London: Routledge.

Craft, A. (2002) *Creativity and Early Years Education*, London: Continuum.

Daniels, H. (ed.) (1993) *Charting the Agenda: Educational Activity after Vygotsky*, London: Routledge.

David, T. (1999) *Young Children Learning*, London: Paul Chapman Publishing.

David, T., Curtis, A. and Siraj-Blatchford, I. (1993) *Effective Teaching in the Early Years: Fostering Children's Learning in Nurseries and Infant Classes*, an OMEP (UK) Report, University of Warwick.

Davies, B. (1987) 'The accomplishment of genderedness in pre-school children', in A. Pollard (ed.) *Children and Their Primary Schools, a New Perspective*, London: Falmer Press.

DES (Department of Education and Science) (1985) *The Curriculum from 5 to 16: Curriculum Matters 2*, London: HMSO.

DES (Department of Education and Science) (1989) *Aspects of Education: The Education of Children under Five*, London: HMSO.

DES (Department of Education and Science) (1990) *Starting with Quality. Report of the Committee of Enquiry into the Quality of the Educational Experience Offered to 3 and 4 Year Olds*, London: HMSO.

DfEE (Department for Education and Employment) (1998a) *Meeting the Childcare Challenge. Green Paper*, London: HMSO.

DfEE (Department for Education and Employment) (1998b) *Circular 4/98, Teaching: High Status, High Standards*, London: DfEE.

Dowling, M. (1995) *Starting School at Four: A Joint Endeavour*, London: Paul Chapman Publishing.

Dowling, M. (2000) *Young Children's Personal, Social and Emotional Development*, London: Paul Chapman Publishing.

Drummond, M.J. (2000) 'Comparisons in early years education: history, fact and fiction', *Early Childhood Research and Practice*, **2**, 1, Spring. Online. Available HTTP: ‹http://www.ecrp.uiuc.edu/v2nl/drummond.html›.

Drummond, M.J. (2002) 'Whatever next? Future trends in early years education', in D. Whitebread (ed.) *Teaching and Learning in the Early Years*, London: Routledge Falmer, pp. 335–347.

Drury, R., Miller, L. and Campbell, R. (2000) *Looking at Early Years Education and Care*, London: David Fulton Publishers.

Edwards, C., Gandini, L. and Forman, G. (1998) *The Hundred Languages of Children. The Reggio Emilia Approach: Advanced Reflections*, 2nd edn, London: Ablex Publishing.

Egan, K. (1988) *Primary Understanding. Education in Early Childhood*, London: Routledge.

Elliott, J. (1980) *The Theory and Practice of Educational Action Research*, Classroom Action Research Network, Bulletin no. 4, Cambridge, Institute of Education.

Elliott, J. (1985) 'Facilitating action research in schools: some dilemmas', in R. Burgess (ed.) *Field Methods in the Study of Education*, Lewes: Falmer Press, pp. 235–262.

Faulkner, D. and Miell, D. (1993) 'Settling in to school: the importance of early friendships for the development of children's social understanding and communicative competence', *International Journal of Early Years Education*, **1**, 23–45

Filer, A. and Pollard, A. (2000) *The Social World of Pupil Assessment*, London: Continuum.

Fisher, J. (2002) *Starting from the Child*, 2nd edn, Buckingham: Open University Press.

Fitz-Gibbon, C.T. and Stephenson-Forster, N.J. (1999) 'Is Ofsted helpful?', in C. Cullingford (ed.) *An Inspector Calls. Ofsted and Its Effects on School Standards*, London: Kogan Page.

Gardner, H. (1983) *Frames of Mind: The Theory of Multiple Intelligences*, New York: Basic Books.

Gardner, H. (1993) *The Unschooled Mind: How Children Think and How Schools Should Teach*, London: Fontana.

Gardner, H. (1998) 'Foreword: complementary perspectives on Reggio Emilia', in Edwards *et al.* (1998), pp. xv–xviii.

Goleman, D. (1998) *Working with Emotional Intelligence*, London: Bloomsbury.

Gura, P. (ed.) (1992) *Exploring Learning. Young Children and Block Play*, London: Paul Chapman Publishing.

Handy, C. (1997) 'Schools for life and work', in *Living Education: Essays in Honour of John Tomlinson*, London: Paul Chapman Publishing.

Hay, D.F. (1994) 'Pro-social development', *Journal of Child Psychology and Psychiatry*, **35**, 29–72.

Head, J. (1999) *Understanding the Boys*, London: Falmer Press.

Hendy, L. and Toon, L. (2001) *Supporting Drama and Imaginative Play in the Early Years*, Buckingham: Open University Press.

Holly, P. and Southworth, G. (1989) *The Developing School*, Lewes: Falmer Press.

Hutt, S.J., Tyler, S., Hutt, C. and Christopherson, H. (1989) *Play, Exploration and Learning: A Natural History of Pre-school*, London: Routledge.

Ivic, I. (1994) 'Lev S. Vygotsky', *Prospects: The Quarterly Review of Comparative Education*, **24**, 3/4, 471–485.

Jackson, C. (2002) '"Laddishness" as a self-worth protection strategy', *Gender and Education*, **14**, 1, 37–51.

Jackson, C. and Warin, J. (2000) 'The importance of gender as an aspect of identity at key transition points in compulsory education', *British Educational Research Journal*, **26**, 3, 375–391.

Jeffery, B. and Woods, P. (1996) 'Feeling de-professionalised: the social construction of emotions during an Ofsted inspection', *Cambridge Journal of Education*, **26**, 3, 325–343.

Jeffery, B. and Woods, P. (1998) *Testing Teachers*, London: Falmer Press.

Johnson, J., Christie, J. and Yawkey, T. (1999) *Play and Early Childhood Development*, 2nd edn, New York: Longman.

Jordan, D.W. and Le Metais, J. (1997) 'Social skilling through cooperative learning', *Educational Research*, **39**, 1, 3–21.

Katz, L.G. (1995) 'What can we learn from Reggio Emilia?', in C. Edwards and G. Forman (eds) *The Hundred Languages of Children*, London: Ablex Publishing, pp. 21–45.

Kaye, K. and Fogel, A. (1980) 'The temporal structure of face-to-face communication between mothers and infants', *Developmental Psychology*, **16**, 454–464.

Kemmis, S. (1981) *The Professional Development of Teachers through Involvement in Action Research Projects*, Geelong: Deakin University

Laevers, F. (1993) 'Deep level learning – an exemplary application on the area of physical knowledge', *European Early Childhood Education Research Journal*, **1**, 1, 53–68.

Laevers, F. (ed.) (1994) *The Innovative Project 'Experiential Education' and the Definition of Quality in Education*, Leuven: Katholieke Universiteit.

Laevers, F. (ed.) (1996) *An Exploration of the Concept of Involvement as an Indicator for Quality in Early Childhood Education*, Dundee: Scottish Consultative Council on the Curriculum.

Lomax, P. (ed.) (1989) *The Management of Change*, Clevedon: Multilingual Matters.

MacMullin, C. (1994) 'The importance of social skills', paper presented at University of Tasmania, Hobart, Tasmania, April.

MacNamara, A. (1995) 'Mathematics', in A. Anning (ed.) *A National Curriculum for the Early Years*, Buckingham: Open University Press, pp. 33–45.

MacNamara, A. (1996) 'From home to school – do children preserve their counting skills?', in P. Broadhead (ed.) *Researching the Early Years Continuum*, Clevedon: Multilingual Matters, pp. 118–127.

MacNaughton, G. (2000) *Rethinking Gender in Early Childhood Education*, London: Paul Chapman Publishing.

Main, M., Kaplan, N. and Cassidy, J. (1985) 'Security in infancy, childhood and adulthood: a move to the level of representation', in I. Bretherton and E.F.Waters (eds) *Growing Points of Attachment Theory and Research*, Monographs of the Society for Research in Child Development, **50** (1–2, serial no. 209).

Marsh, J. (1999) 'Batman and Batwoman go to school: popular culture in the literacy curriculum', *International Journal of Early Years Education*, **7**, 2, 117–131.

Marsh, J. (2000) 'But I want to fly too!': girls and superhero play in the infant classroom', *Gender and Education*, **12**, 2, 209–220.

Miller, L. (2001) 'Shaping early childhood through the literacy curriculum', *Early Years*, **21**, 2, 107–116.

Moss, P. (2001) 'The otherness of Reggio', in L. Abbott and C. Nutbrown (eds) *Experiencing Reggio Emilia: Implications for Pre-school Provision*, Buckingham: Open University Press, pp. 125–137.

Moss, P. and Pence, A. (eds) (1994) *Valuing Quality in Early Childhood Services*, London: Paul Chapman Publishing.

Moss, P. and Penn, H. (1996) *Transforming Nursery Education*, London: Paul Chapman Publishing.

National Commission on Education (1993) *Learning to Succeed*, London: Heinemann.

Nias, J. and Groundwater-Smith, S. (eds) (1988) *The Enquiring Teacher: Supporting and Sustaining Teacher Research*, Lewes: Falmer Press.

Nutbrown, K. (1994) *Threads of Thinking*, London: Paul Chapman Publishing.

Oberhuemer, P. and Ulich, M. (1997) *Working with Young Children in Europe*, London: Paul Chapman Publishing.

O'Flaherty, J. (1995) *Intervening in the Early Years: An Evaluation of the High/Scope Curriculum*, London: National Children's Bureau.

OfSTED (1995) *Guidance on the Inspection of Nursery and Primary Schools*, London: HMSO.

Oja, S.N. and Smulyan, L. (1989) *Collaborative Action Research: A Developmental Approach*, Lewes: Falmer Press.

Pascal, C. (1990) *Under Fives in the Infant classroom*, Stoke-on-Trent: Trentham.

Pascal, C., Bertram, A.D. and Ramsden, F. (1994) *Effective Early Learning: The Quality Evaluation and Development Process*, Worcester: Amber Publications.

Pascal, C., Bertram, A.D., Ramsden, F., Georgeson, J., Saunders, M. and Mould, C. (1995) *Effective Early Learning: Evaluating and Developing Quality in Early Childhood Settings*, Worcester: Amber Publications.

Pascal, C., Bertram, A.D., Ramsden, F., Georgeson, J., Saunders, M. and Mould, C. (1996) *Evaluating and Developing Quality in Early Childhood Settings: A Professional Development Programme*, Worcester: Amber Publications.

Pipp, S., Easterbrooks M.A. and Brown, S.R. (1993) 'Attachment status and complexity of infants' self and other knowledge when tested with mother and father', *Social Development*, **2**, 1–14.

QCA (2000) *Curriculum Guidance for the Foundation Stage*, Sudbury: QCA Publications.

QCA (2003) *Foundation Stage Profile*, Sudbury: QCA Publications.

Rahman, M., Palmer, G., Kenway, P. and Howarth, C. (2000) *Monitoring Poverty and Social Exclusion*, York: Joseph Rowntree Foundation.

Rhinegold, H.L. (1982) 'Little children's participation in the world of adults, a nascent pro-social behaviour', *Child Development*, **46**, 459–463.

Rogers, S. (1998) 'Play: a conflict of interests? Researching teachers' perceptions of role play as an educational activity in mainstream settings', paper presented at the Annual Conference of the British Educational Research Association, Belfast.

Roskos, K. and Christie, J. (2001) 'Examining the play–literacy interface: a critical review and future directions', *Journal of Early Childhood Literacy*, **1**, 1 59–89.

Schaffer, H.R. (1996) *Social Development*, Oxford: Blackwell.

Schneider-Rosen, K. and Cicchetti, D. (1984) 'The relationship between affect and cognition in maltreated infants: quality of attachment and the development of self-recognition', *Child Development*, **55**, 648–658.

Schweinhart, L.J., Barnes, H.V. and Weikart, D.P. (1993) *Significant Benefits: The High/Scope Perry Preschool Project through age 27*, Ypsilenti, MI: The High/Scope Press.

Simons, H. (1987) *Getting to Know Schools in a Democracy, the Politics and Process of Evaluation*, Lewes: Falmer Press.

Siraj-Blatchford, I. (1993) 'Objectional objectivity', *Early Years*, **13**, 2, Spring, 50–53.

Smith, C. (1998) 'Children with "special rights" in the preprimary schools and infant-toddler centres of Reggio Emilia', in Edwards *et al.* (1998), pp. 199–214.

Stenhouse, L. (1975) *An Introduction to Curriculum Research and Development*, London: Heinemann.

Stephen, C. and Wilkinson, E. (1999) 'Rhetoric and reality in developing language and mathematical skill: plan and playroom experience', *Early Years*, **19**, 2, 62–73.

Stern, D.N. (1998) *The Interpersonal World of the Infant*, London: Karnac Books.

Sylva, K. (1991) 'Educational aspects of day care in England and Wales', in P. Moss and E. Melhuish (eds) *Current Issues in Day Care for Young Children*, London: HMSO.

Sylva, K., Pascal, C., Pugh, G. and Duffy, B. (1999a) 'Frameworks for learning', *RSA Journal*, **CXLVI** (5488), 107–112.

Sylva, K., Sammons, P., Melhuish, E.C., Siraj-Blatchford, I., Taggart, B., Dobson, A., Jeavons, M., Lewis, K., Morahan, M. and Sadler, S. (1999b) 'Introduction to the Effective Provision of Pre-School Education Project', *The Effective Provision of Pre-school Education Project, Technical Paper 1* (EPPE Project), London: DfEE/Institute of Education.

Thorne, B. (1993) *Gender Play: Girls and Boys in School*, Buckingham: Open University Press.

Thumpston, G. and Whitehead, M. (1994) 'The impact of testing at Key Stage 1: some early research evidence', in G.M. Blenkin and A.V. Kelly (eds) *The National Curriculum and Early Learning*, London: Paul Chapman Publishing, pp. 66–86.

Vygotsky, L.S. (1962) *Thought and Language*, translated by E. Hanfmann and G. Vakar, Cambridge, MA: MIT Press.

Vygotsky, L.S. (1976) 'Play and its role in the mental development of the child', in J. Bruner, A. Jolly and K. Sylva (eds) *Play: Its Role in Development and Evolution*, New York: Basic Books, pp. 537–554.

Vygotsky, L.S. (1978) *Mind in Society: The Development of Higher Psychological Processes*, London: Harvard University Press.

Vygotsky, L.S. (1986) *Thought and Language*, translation revised and edited by A. Kozulin, Cambridge, MA: MIT Press.

Walkerdine, V. (1989) *Counting Girls Out*, London: Virago.

Walkerdine, V. (1997) *Daddy's Girl: Young Girls and Popular Culture*, London: Macmillan.

Wallace, M. (1991) 'Coping with multiple innovations in school: an exploratory study', *Educational Management and Administration*, **19**, 3, 180–192.

Webb, R. (ed.) (1990) *Practitioner Research in the Primary School*, Lewes: Falmer Press.

Whitehead, J. (1985) 'An analysis of an individual's educational development: the basis for personally orientated action research', in M. Shipman (ed.) *Educational Research: Principles, Policies and Practices*, London: Falmer Press.

Wood, E. (2000) 'The roots of under-achievement of boys in literacy in the early years', paper presented at the British Educational Research Association Annual Conference, Cardiff.

Wood, E. and Attfield, J. (1996) *Play, Learning and the Early Childhood Curriculum*, London: Paul Chapman Publishing.

Wood, E. and Bennett, N. (2000) 'Changing theories, changing practice: exploring early childhood teachers' professional learning', *Teaching and Teacher Education*, **16**, 635–647.

Zahn-Waxler, C., Radke-Yarrow, M., Wagner, E. and Chapman, M. (1992) 'Development of concern for others', *Developmental Psychology*, **28**, 126–136.

Index